the verve

crazed highs + horrible lows

martin clarke

plexus, london

Copyright © 1998 by Independent Music Press
Published by Plexus Publishing Limited
55a Clapham Common Southside
London SW4 9BX
First Printing 1998

British Library Cataloguing in Publication Data

Clarke, Martin
    The Verve : crazed highs and horrible
    lows
    1. Verve (Group) 2. Rock musicians -
    Great Britain - Biography
    I. Title
    782.4'2'166'0922

    ISBN 0 85965 263 7

Cover and book design by Phil Gambrill
Printed in Great Britain by Hillman Printers
(Frome) Ltd

10 9 8 7 6 5 4 3 2 1

Acknowledgements
The following journalists, articles and publications
proved invaluable to the completion of this book
and provide excellent sources for all fans. The
author would like to express his thanks for their
work: NME: 24/10/92 Live Review by Stuart
Maconie; 29/02/92 Live review by Gina Morris;
08/02/92 Live review by John Mulvey; 09/05/92
Live review by Roger Morton; 20/06/92 Feature
by Roger Morton; 27/06/92 Live review by John
Mulvey; 25/07/92 Live review by Johnny
Cigarettes; 17/10/92 Feature; 03/07/93 Live
review; 15/05/93 Feature by Steve Sutherland;
06/05/95 Singles review; 13/05/95 Feature;
10/06/95 Singles review;17/06/95 Live review by
Paul Moody; 24/06/95 Feature; 07/06/97 Feature;
21/06/97 News; 23/08/97 Feature; 27/09/97
album Review Ted Kessler; 22/11/97 Feature by
Sylvia Patterson; 24/01/98; 7/2/98. Melody
Maker: 10/10/92 Live review; 20/06/92 live
review Paul Lester; 17/10/92 Live review Ian
Gittens; 15/05/93 Singles review Ian Gittens;
29/05/93 Live review, Simon Price; 19/06/93 LP
Review David Stubbs; 10/09/94 Live review Ian
Watson; 28/05/94 LP/EP Review A. Smith;
03/09/94 Live review; 29/04/95 Live review M.
Bonner; 29/04/95 Singles review;13/05/95
Feature; 03/06/95 Feature Tom Doyle; 24/06/95
Singles review; 01/07/95 Album review; 15/07/95
Feature Simon Price; 16/08/97 News; 30/08/97
Feature RB; 11/10/97 Feature Jade Gordon;
29/11/97 Feature Paul Mathews; 17/01/98 Robin
Bresnak. 17/08/98 The Observer Barbara Ellen;
The Observer The Verve by William Leith;
01/09/97 The Scotsman Feature by Barrie
Didcock; 14/09/97 Scotland On Sunday Charles
McFaulds; 10/97 VOX Feature by Sylvia
Patterson; 11/97 Q Feature; 16/01/98 Eye On
Friday; Evening Standard Live Review by Max
Bell; 20/01/98 The Sun Feature; 03/98 Q Feature.
The Sun, The Daily Telegraph, The Guardian,
The Observer, The Times, Daily Mirror,
Independent on Sunday, The Independent,
Rolling Stone magazine, The Sunday Times, The
Radio Times. The finest article on The Verve to
date is Martin Aston's superb feature in Select,
03/98.
    Thanks to the following photographers/ agen-
cies for supplying pictures: Richard Beland/S.I.N.;
Melanie Cox/S.I.N.; Jeffrey Davy/S.I.N.; Steve
Double/S.I.N.; Greg Freeman/S.I.N.; Liane
Hentschet/S.I.N.; Angela Lubrano; Magnolia
Press/All Action; Sue Moore/All Action; Phil
Nicholls/S.I.N.; Tim Paton/S.I.N.; Roger
Sargent/Rex Features; Gene Shaw/All Action.
Justin Thomas/All Action. Cover photograph by
Roger Sargent, Rex Features.

contents

a serious boy

'It's not that small, but it's small in terms of having any social night-life or gathering. It's great if you wear patent leather shoes and drink nineteen pints of lager; you'll have the time of your life.'
richard ashcroft

For a band whose early reputation would centre on discussing the merits of spiritual travel, telekinesis and meditation, there could be few less glamorous localities in which to be raised than Wigan, or, more specifically, the mundane suburb of Billinge. Perhaps not surprisingly, this small town had no previous musical legacy, and Wigan itself had only a passing claim to fame. Admittedly, there was a thriving northern soul scene in its darkest clubs, but otherwise the closest it got to musical notoriety was with the window-cleaning, ukulele-playing George Formby in the thirties and forties. Other than that, Wigan possessed a renowned Rugby League team, a legendary casino and a gargantuan Heinz baked bean factory.

Located as it is in the north-west of the metropolitan area of Greater Manchester, Wigan lies along the River Douglas and the Leeds and Liverpool Canal, which in the eighteenth century provided excellent facilities for, initially, a thriving cotton trade, which was usurped in the nineteenth century by an equally successful coal industry. After the Second World War, however, Wigan received an influx of newer industries, most notably food processing, paper packaging, electrical and general engineering. Thus the baked bean factory, filled with local shift workers, provided an uninspiring source of income for large chunks of the 300,000-strong native population.

Of course, to a young Richard Ashcroft, none of this mattered. The eldest of three children (he had two younger sisters, Victoria and Laura), he was a striking looking lad, with a large nose and a gaunt face perched on a painfully thin body. The nose was inherited from his father Frank, whose job as an office clerk meant that family life was suitably mundane and stable. During his first ten years, the only real drama came with Richard's constant visits to the family doctor with a variety of minor ailments, as a result of which he was eventually told, 'You're going to have a cold for the rest of your life, so you'd better get used to it.' Then, when Richard was only eleven, his father suffered a freak brain haemorrhage, when a dormant blood clot caused by a car crash in his teens suddenly exploded with fatal consequences. It was, understandably, an event that was to have enormous and long-lasting effects on Richard's formative years and, indeed, his adulthood.

'The first thing they told us *was* that George Best *was* a prick! *Well*, I wasn't having that. I mean, come on! He had *two* blondes before the Chelsea game and still scored!'

The immediate effect was to make him a very dour and overly serious child: 'Other kids were playing with their Action Men and I was questioning life and society.' In time, however, the precious nature of life dawned on Richard, and this in turn created an impulse in him to break free of the suffocating lifestyle that seemed to envelop his local community. He later told *Select*, '[My Dad] worked nine to five and got nowhere. I immediately realised that wasn't the life for me . . . That one moment of realisation made a mockery of any authority from then on.

I gained an awareness of how quickly people can leave you and how little time you've got to enjoy yourself and show yourself off and have relationships with people . . . I thought, "Fuck this, I'm gonna make something special of myself."'

After his father died, Richard quickly developed into a notoriously loud and outspoken boy at Upholland Comprehensive School, even earning the nickname 'Jesus' because of his constant desire to be the centre of attention. Matched with his general uninterest in academia, this trait made Richard an unpopular pupil with the teaching staff, one of whom tastelessly berated him as 'the cancer of the class'. Richard found his escape from this in sport, particularly football, at which he excelled. By the age of thirteen he was one of the best in the school team, Upholland FC, and the following season he was good enough to be playing in the adult pub team league at weekends, where, despite his spindly frame and poor lung capacity, he was a capable and respected player. This resulted in him enrolling for the Bobby Charlton Soccer School. His excitement at this, as an avid Manchester United fan, was soon punctured when the coaches there immediately criticised his all-time hero: 'The first thing they told us was that George Best was a prick! Well, I wasn't having that. I mean, come on! He had two blondes before the Chelsea game and still scored!'

Unfortunately, Richard had a mouth to match his expanding ego (which had earned him a broken nose on four occasions), and this proved to be his downfall. The school games teacher tired of his attitude, and as Richard was also losing enthusiasm for soccer and was suffering from painful knees, the sport was soon replaced with another obsession: music.

Like many teenagers in the mid-1980s, Richard's first real musical love was the Smiths, although he never fully joined the gladioli-waving ranks of Morrissey fanatics. He had little money to buy singles, so spent many hours with his tape recorder, waiting for the radio to play his favourite songs. His tastes quickly became eclectic, including the likes of James Brown, Otis Redding, Sly and the Family Stone, and Iggy Pop, as well as a host of more contemporary artists. Since his father's death, Richard had sworn never to be shackled to a day job in the same way, and music offered him a potential escape. He decided the first move was to tell his careers teacher, who listened with resignation before sending him to the local swimming baths for a couple of weeks' work experience as a lifeguard. When he arrived at the chlorine-drenched Wigan Baths, Richard revealed he had not even earned a 25-metre swimming badge. Combined with his eight-stone frame this hardly made him an ideal lifesaver, so he was duly assigned to maintenance, which was a thinly veiled title for cleaning the toilets. 'I went from an Adonis in a big high chair to scrubbing bogs. So I thought: "That's enough of this work business – fuck it."' It was to be Richard's sole brush with a normal working life.

This nasty work experience only fuelled his desire to make it in music, even though at this stage he couldn't play a note. For the time being, he revelled in a pseudo-pop star personality, strutting around the school with a new haircut every few weeks, courtesy of his hairdresser mother (she stills cuts hair for a living). In the space of one year alone his lanky, cocky frame modelled a perm, a bleached bowl and blond streaks. In an attempt at 'an Andy Warhol' he accidentally turned his hair purple, and he then tried to dye it black, but instead it turned blue. He later admitted to also having a 'big Shakin' Stevens dyed black hairdo with sideburns down to here, [and] even the early eighties permed-at-the-back footballer's cut. Yes! I was that lad.'

By now, Richard's love of music was proving to be a serious distraction to his school work. Once while sitting a test in philosophy and religion, Richard found himself bored with the exam paper and, enticed by the sunny weather outside, simply got up and walked out. When he had not reappeared hours later, the school authorities were so concerned they had the local canal dredged. Clearly confused by his attitude, the teachers suggested that he see a psychiatrist. Richard refused.

Richard was firmly established as an outsider. This status was thoroughly encouraged by the views of the man who became Richard's mother's new husband. A former teacher, the new stepfather had views that were unorthodox to say the least. For a start, he was a follower of the Rosicrucians. The origins of this early sixteenth-century movement are rather obscure, but at its nucleus is a brotherhood who claim to possess an esoteric wisdom that has been handed down from ancient times. Indeed, the reputed father of their ideas, Christian Rosenkreuz, who is said to have lived for 106 years, formed the basis of the philosophy on travels to Egypt and Arabia. Richard's stepfather was heavily immersed in these beliefs, and regularly talked about astral travel, chaos theory, inner discovery and telekinesis. By his sixteenth birthday, Richard was telling his bemused friends how his stepdad could bend light rays around people so as to make

Verve: An early group shot of the band before they adopted the definite article, with Richard Ashcroft very much at the forefront.

them vanish. He also proudly explained that when his stepfather's business was struggling, he imagined strangers sending him cheques, and soon after money started arriving in the post. Richard claimed to have seen this man raise the temperature in a room just by thinking about it (so-called 'creative visualisation'), and said that he himself had once heard people whistling twenty miles away.

Richard's stepfather supported him and helped build his confidence, buying him a motorbike and unreservedly encouraging his love of music. He went on to write a biography of Alfred Bestall, author of the Rupert Bear stories, and his role in Richard's formative teenage years is clearly pivotal, with The Verve frontman describing him as both 'a genius and a guru'. Having said that, he would never fill the enormous vacuum left by the death of his biological father: 'I can never balance out what I've lost. But in the end you are on your own. You can be in love, or married or feel really attached to something, but in the end you are on your own. I believe that.'

Encouraged by this liberal environment, Richard set about forming a band. Also taking the aforementioned philosophy and religion exam were two of Richard's school friends, Simon Jones and Pete Salisbury. Salisbury, known as Sobbo, first squared up to Richard in the school yard, and the following year a crunching Ashcroft tackle broke his ankle during a school football match. Inspired by Richard's brazen arrogance and wild enthusiasm for music, Simon started playing guitar, as he later told *Exclaim!* magazine: 'I take my hat off to him, 'cause I remember being a school boy . . . and me asking him, "What yer gonna do when school is done?" like you do to your mate, and he's like, "Oh, I'm gonna be a singer in a band," and I'm going "Yeah, yeah, yeah." We couldn't even fucking play a note, but he's always thought like that.'

With barely a handful of GCSEs between them, Richard, Sobbo and Simon headed for Winstanley Sixth Form College (Richard's natural intelligence had helped him through a few exams, despite his utter lack of application). Also in their gang was Simon Tong, a long-time friend who had taught Simon and Richard their very first guitar chords. Meanwhile, Richard's parents had moved to the Cotswolds, but Richard opted to stay behind, rooming with Jones for much of the time they were at college together. At that college, Richard befriended a quiet and reserved lad in the year above, from neighbouring St Helens, by the name of

Nick McCabe. Nick was a responsible, pensive and shy boy, but never got picked on because of the reputation of his elder brother Paul, who had been in prison three times by his fifteenth birthday, including one time for stealing three cars and being involved in a police chase around the Birmingham motorway system.

In sharp contrast to Nick's introversion, Richard was brimming with confidence and cocksure arrogance. Despite being such opposites, the two outsiders hit it off quickly, and became firm friends. Nick was already a competent guitarist, and his own band was in dire need of a good singer. He speculatively played some tracks to Richard in the college practice room, and, suitably impressed, Richard immediately joined, recalling later that the songs sounded like 'a whole other universe to me'. The fairly loose line-up, regularly featuring a drum machine, played only a handful of gigs, which largely proved to be a vehicle for Richard's penchant for outrageous live performances. Parading under various monickers such as the Butterfly Effect and Raingarden, most of their shows were in the college canteen at lunch times to an uninterested crowd of fellow pupils. This did not deter Richard's energetic tendencies: 'At the end of one show,' Richard later confessed to *Select*, 'I just completely freaked out and started rolling on the floor. These kids were staring at me, going, "What a wanker – what the fuck is he doing?" My friends thought I'd cracked. But I just couldn't help it.' Despite this enthusiasm, the band soon fell apart, but Nick and Richard continued to write and rehearse together.

The other future members of The Verve had also been involved in various bands at college. Sobbo had been drumming in a marching band, and then later for a group called the Comedians. Both Simon Tong and Simon Jones were members of a band called Laughing Gravy, which then became Applecart, but neither line-up was to enjoy any longevity. The five friends formed a rowdy gang away from their music, and would often walk up to the Beacon, the park on the outskirts of Wigan, getting blind drunk on cheap Thunderbird and Special Brew. They would often take a tape player with them, shattering the solitude and peace of the surrounding countryside. As classmate Chas Chandler recalled in *Select*, they were 'a lively crowd, having a laugh and doing as little work as possible . . . They were into their music, though. They listened to Can and Funkadelic even then, to Zeppelin and the Stones, and, of course, the Stone Roses, everyone's favourite.'

The spring of 1989 heralded the beginnings of 'Madchester' when the Mancunian bands would revolutionise the rock and dance format, following in the tradition of Joy Division, New Order and various lesser-known acts such as A Certain Ratio. The Stone Roses led the way, with the Happy Mondays and Inspiral Carpets following closely behind, as 'baggy' music swept the nation up in a tide of flares, shirts with extra long sleeves and Joe Bloggs clothing. There was a general air of apathy around these bands, arising from drugs, inactivity and an apolitical and abstract dismay towards life. The eponymous debut album from Ian Brown's Stone Roses was rightly hailed as a classic, while the shambling, drug-addled Happy Mondays' long player, *Pills, Thrills And Bellyaches* reinforced the party atmosphere of this new scene. However, by the end of the next year, 'baggy' would be dead creatively, with its foremost proponents, the Stone Roses, locked in bitter courtroom struggles. For now, though, 1989 belonged to them and their fellow Manchester groups.

'My youth has been strangulated [in *Wigan*]. That's the main reason *why we* started a band – to enjoy our youth *whilst we've* got it, seeing places *whilst we're* fit and *whilst we're* living.'

As keen music lovers, it was impossible for Richard and his mates to ignore this scene – indeed, they loved it. As Richard later recalled to *Time Out*, 'Back in the eighties, whenever you turned on the TV it was Phil Collins, it was Robert Palmer, it was Peter-fucking-Gabriel – all these people who were in something before you were conscious! It was like, "Who are these geezers with suits on who keep getting big hits, mum?" When I saw the Happy Mondays and the Stone Roses, it was a revelation.' He also loved the Charlatans, whose 'The Only One I Know' single was a key piece in the baggy jigsaw. But it was the Stone Roses who carried the flame most inspiringly: 'Seeing them play Warrington in 1989 basically changed my life,' Richard later told *Select*. 'These guys looked and dressed like me and they were from the same background, yet they were onstage, being adored. Seeing them made me realise that I could do that as well. . . I could do better.'

Buoyed by this new British music scene, Richard was more keen than ever to make things happen. At this point, his life consisted largely of waking up late in the day, getting stoned and then going back to bed. It was mind-numbing: 'My youth has been strangulated [in Wigan]. That's the main reason why we started a band – to enjoy our youth whilst we've got it, seeing places whilst we're fit and whilst we're living.' One night when he was driving in the dark lanes around Wigan with Simon Jones, he finally decided to take action: 'Looking at the lights, I thought to myself that out of those millions of lights, not one of them knows me and we're just fucking rotting away on the dole doing nothing. That was the first spark.' Recruiting Sobbo, Nick and Simon Jones, they christened themselves Verve, 'a good name, [it] means excitement and emotion'. Supported by their weekly Social Security cheques, Verve started to rehearse hard.

Their first gig was on 15 August 1990 at the Honeysuckle pub in Poolstock, outside Wigan, where they played just two songs for the birthday celebrations of Richard's flatmate, Paul Frodsham. Watched by a small crowd, which included their good friend Dave Halliwell (who would soon become their manager), Verve played basic but interesting tracks by the names of 'The Sun, The Sea' and 'Your Back'. At this stage, Simon's bass playing was so rudimentary that he had to memorise his lines, and when the band veered off into a brief improvised ramble (as they would soon become renowned for), he was totally lost. He was forced to wait until the music came back round to a section he could recognise before joining in again. Interestingly, the DJ for the night was their friend, Wayne Griggs, alias Spheres of Music, who would later spin the records before all Verve gigs.

Despite their enthusiasm, Verve did not play live again for another year, partly because of their lack of original material and partly because of a lack of direction. Eventually Richard contemplated this lack of progress and decided to take control. The next day, he phoned Sobbo, who was now studying Ceramics and Geology at Stoke Polytechnic. He then tracked Nick down in Liverpool, where he was training as a quantity surveyor. After listening to Richard rant about the band's potential, both friends jacked in their respective career paths immediately. With Simon still involved, and Halliwell now officially acting as band manger, Verve took the first steps on what was to prove a bizarre, lengthy and tempestuous journey.

highs and lows

'I want The Verve to be the biggest band in the world because rock 'n' roll will will be dangerous again if we are.'
richard ashcroft

Funded by the Department of Health and Social Security's benevolence, and a few pounds garnered from sales of rehearsal tapes to supportive friends, Verve booked their second gig, at the famous Manchester Boardwalk, on 3 February 1991. Although they were still a shambolic, albeit energetic affair, the local newspaper, the *Wigan Reporter*, noted that 'they were cooking on gas . . . [and] singer Richard had the crowd of over 200 eating out of the palm of his hand'. The *Wigan Reporter* later ran a headline declaring 'Band War Breaks Out' after Verve struck up a rivalry with fellow Wigan band the Tansads, with Richard denying their support slot to the latter was any indication of their potential, saying instead it was a chance 'to show Wigan who's boss'. For the best part of the year, Verve gigged sporadically in the North-West, and quickly earned a solid reputation for their live shows at venues such as the Citadel in St. Helens and The Bolton Institute Students Union. Rehearsals at Splash Studios were interspersed with small club gigs, which already featured the lengthy jams, often lasting as long as 30 minutes, that were to become a Verve trademark. This improvisational style was largely inspired by the likes of Can, Sly and the Family Stone, and Funkadelic.

Already the band were using drugs openly and extravagantly, sometimes to encourage their muse, other times for the sake of it: 'We are really serious about the band, but we're also relaxed. We don't have set practice times, we just get together and jam and try to mould a song out of it. The actual construction of the songs is really natural. It rolls.' Many post-gig parties were thus enjoyed suitably stoned on the top of the Beacon, dropping acid and dancing around forest bonfires, at the same spot where, only a few years before, the fifteen-year-old friends had met to get pissed and dream of being in a rock 'n' roll band. Richard called this lifestyle 'the whole experience'. More gigs at the Boardwalk followed, and within months the local press had them earmarked as potential new stars, calling them 'gigantic' and 'already immortal'. They were yet to release a record.

With this in mind, Richard organised a demo session, funded through the foresight of a small Norwich-based record label called Backs, and actually recorded in the living room of Simon's parents. Despite such a primitive environment, the tape captured promising and heavily psychedelic versions of 'All In The Mind', 'The Sun, The Sea', 'Slide Away' and 'Verve Arising'. With this tape in hand, Verve headed south for their debut London show. They had deliberately delayed this experience of the capital: 'If you come from London,' Richard explained to *Melody Maker*, 'you've got people coming down to see you from the word go and writing you off too early, whereas we've had years . . . I've been in bands since I was seventeen. We've had years to get it ready. And only when we were ready did we play a gig in London. We played one gig in London and we were signed up.'

This gig was on 3 July 1991, at the King's Head pub in Fulham, in front of only a handful of people, one of whom was David Boyd, label boss of Hut Records, a subsidiary signed to Virgin Records which counted the Smashing Pumpkins amongst its charges. Verve were third on the bill to an obscure and soon-to-be-forgotten jazz fusion band. Boyd would later go on record as saying 'meeting The Verve changed my life', and even at this stage, despite the band's musical phylogeny, he was convinced. His label scout, Miles Leonard, had already heard Verve's demo and was sufficiently excited enough to travel up north to see one of their

Boardwalk gigs. Convinced the band were right for Hut, he had arranged the Fulham gig, but was rather concerned to hear that Sony and Polydor were also sniffing around the young band after a second, better demo had been mailed out. 'Their demo was so much better than anything else I was hearing,' Leonard told *Select* magazine. 'Richard was already a complete star. The band was so innovative.' Boyd agreed: 'I smelt and heard Verve rather than just seeing them. Richard was climbing the monitors . . . It was classic rock 'n' roll, like, "What's going to happen next, will he break his neck or what?" I saw within two songs what their potential was.' Verve signed to Hut Records in September 1991. They had been officially together for just twelve months.

* * *

'When we signed a deal, we got a stash of money. I rented a flat in Wigan and in that flat we just had the most ridiculously indulgent, decadent six months. Now all the money's gone and I'm totally skint – but it was a good time.'
richard ashcroft

Unfortunately, Hut Records' enthusiasm for Verve was not matched by their seniors at Virgin Records. Several meetings were arranged at their London headquarters, but Virgin did not even offer to pay for the band's travel and accommodation. Consequently, Hut's Miles Leonard broke into a squat near his Ladbroke Grove home and let the band stay there, where they would crash in sleeping bags before meeting the inhospitable Virgin executives the next day. Once back in Wigan, Verve's advance from the record deal was quickly squandered on drugs, food, beer and, apparently lasagne, which Richard had delivered to his door every day for six months. At this stage, Verve's non-prescription drug intake was fairly massive, and when they did make it down to London they were not always particularly lucid, as Richard later recalled: 'I remember coming down, walking around . . . in bare feet, like an absolute maniac, with me hair down to me shoulders, fookin' off my head.' He also later described Verve's initial forays to the capital as 'the fuckin' Wiganites, arms aloft in warrior poses, coming over the hills with spears, in loin-cloths'.

While such a chemical intake and wayward lifestyle did not always make for the most professional of meetings, in terms of the band's live performance, this excess seemed to fuel their fire. Their second London show was at the tiny Camden Falcon in the first week of December, supporting Whirlpool. Camden was currently at the centre of what was then a very fashionable scene. Just before grunge, led by Nirvana, took the world by storm, so-called 'shoe-gazing' was trying to maintain a grip on the UK music scene, whereby listless, apolitical and monosyllabic groups like Ride, Moose, the Boo Radleys, Lush, Chapterhouse, Telescopes and Slowdive all performed swirling, effects-laden songs while standing almost completely motionless, eyes fixed on their toes. Whirlpool belonged to this scene, which was also known as 'The Scene That Celebrates Itself'.

So it was clear that Verve's psychedelic ramblings were hardly the current vogue, but the industry whispers about Hut's new signings swelled the Falcon to near capacity. Then came the band's biggest show to date, supporting the Smashing Pumpkins at London's Astoria. Unfortunately, it was also one of their worst shows so far – they complained of having to play too early in the night and without a soundcheck, and once onstage Richard threw the microphone around the floor and smashed a vodka bottle. The promoter pulled the plug after just a few songs – 'they might have turned us off, but we've turned you on,' hailed the singer.

Shortly after another London show at the Tufnell Park Dome, and a debut John Peel session, Verve released their debut single, 'All In The Mind', on 9 March 1992. In the producer's chair was Stone Roses engineer Paul Schroeder, whose laid-back approach allowed them to take control at Impact Studios, a converted barn in Canterbury. What this meant in reality was that huge, debilitating quantities of acid were taken, resulting in all of the initial versions being completely abandoned. The band were studio debutantes, and their frustration at not being able to capture the sounds they heard in their heads caused great distress and yet more narcotic abuse. Eventually, after the drugs had worn off, they were able to complete the three tracks needed.

It was a powerful yet pleasantly wistful debut, hinting at influences from Echo and the Bunnymen as much as any sixties psychedelia, and reviewers name-checked the Rolling Stones, the Byrds, Sonic Youth and even U2 as possible reference points. At the core of the appeal was Richard's cockiness, encapsulated in the line 'She said "You were born to fly my son/I said "Hey, I already know."' All three tracks were dripping with sheer attitude, with the B-sides being arguably far stronger than the lead track. 'A Man Called Sun' was of particular note, with its Doors-ish ramblings clocking in at no less than seven minutes. The track had originally been more controlled, but a prolonged jam in the studio resulted in the final epic take. With the cover artwork showing the band in Wigan's Mesnes Park, complete with a Vespa, some of Richard's furniture and their friend's band the Bed Event, it was a very capable debut.

'Can you imagine what it was like? A blast. Hilarious . . . All of a sudden, it just seemed real. You're in a band and you can actually do things. And someone is paying you.'

During this period, Verve flew to America, where they set up on the back of a truck and drove around Manhattan while playing extended versions of 'A Man Called Sun'. They loved spending long periods around Times Square: 'It was amazing! Everyone was dancing, from the pimps to the prostitutes to the tourists. Everywhere we went, people got into this rhythm and started dancing.' They also played three gigs, and the annual CMJ convention, an industry showcase for new alternative talent. The band were booked into the Chelsea Hotel, where Sid Vicious was arrested for allegedly killing his girlfriend Nancy Spungeon, and where stars such as Jim Morrison, Bob Dylan and Janis Joplin had stayed. To make the atmosphere even more of a party, several of their friends flew over. It was a wild time, as Dave Halliwell later told *Select*: 'For all of us, it was the height of everything. Can you imagine what it was like? A blast. Hilarious . . . All of a sudden, it just seemed real. You're in a band and you can actually do things. And someone is paying you.'

However, back in Britain, they soon had reservations about the debut release ('it was only two or three weeks before we were thinking, "Christ, we could have done it a lot better"'), but with shameless duplicity, Richard later claimed great things for it, describing 'A Man Called Sun' as 'one of the most beautiful things we've ever done, and for it not to be taken as such at the time seemed like a fucking tragedy'. The media folk who

'If I can move
a person emotionally,
and take them to
another place,
it *would* mean
more to me
than being
on *Top Of The Pops*
or seeing us
in the Top Ten'

*From the very first, Verve aimed for parity
with classic performers like the Rolling Stones
or Sly Stone.*

weren't fawning over the current American grunge invasion saw fit to hail this release as a promising volley from a band of considerable potential. *NME* said Verve made 'the idea of the Stone Roses ever making another record seem, well, unnecessary. They will be bigger than drugs.' They also said, 'If nothing more than self-belief sold records, Verve will be breathing down Simply Red's neck in a matter of weeks. No problem.'

'Each slightly awkward and gawky pose is brazenly executed. One in every hundred or so frontmen owns this spark of charisma . . .' *Gina Morris, NME*

On the tour to promote the release, supporting both Ride and Spiritualized, Verve were typically volatile. Gina Morris of the *NME* said, 'Verve are good, very good. They know it and it's no problem. Onstage, Richard conjures up Gillespie/Jagger comparisons; each slightly awkward and gawky pose is brazenly executed. One in every hundred or so frontmen owns this spark of charisma . . .' However, in Norwich, they left the stage after only two songs because they felt the sound wasn't good enough nor the crowd large enough, all this despite having driven in a van for six hours from Wigan the same afternoon ('It wasn't happening, and we explained that to the people afterwards and they understood'). On the same tour, they bored a largely uninterested London crowd at the Town and Country Club with a particularly self-indulgent 25-minute jam, a potentially disastrous mistake in the capital that left their press officer frantic with worry. Fortunately, several reviewers loved it, and the stakes surrounding Verve raised another notch – their momentum was beginning to build.

* * *

At this stage, Virgin Records may well have thought they were on the verge of a new pop sensation. Unfortunately for them, they had not taken full account of Verve's unorthodoxy. The band's very next single was a live favourite, a sprawling *nine-minute* blast called 'She's A Superstar'. A clear signal that Verve held no respect for traditional single formats, the lengthy lead track virtually guaranteed them no radio play and chart failure. With Paul Schroeder's place being taken by Spiritualized producer Bar Clempson (who would also oversee their third single), Verve were audibly more accomplished in the studio. Covered in subtle but weird guitar work by a rapidly improving Nick McCabe, 'She's A Superstar' was perhaps Verve's first true sign of potential greatness, telling tales of high-life, drug-taking and exploitative love, and ending with an extra six minutes of wild, free-form feedback-filled jamming. The band themselves were much happier, and agreed that part of the single's appeal was that it sounded far closer to their live show. Interestingly, the cover artwork, which some people thought was Niagara Falls, was actually a three-foot high waterfall in Snake Pass in Derbyshire, with food colouring used to dye the river to brighten the effect!

Spiritualized

In the current climate of long hair, thrift-store shirts and Sub Pop-inspired minimalism, Verve were asking to be ridiculed, and many sceptical critics aired mocking concerns about prog rock. Such lengthy musical ramblings and lyrical pretension hadn't been fashionable for years. Take, for example, the lines 'Here she comes/Seven suns/A burning flame/

She got my love.' A handful of bands, such as Swervedriver with their anthemic 'Never Lose That Feeling' and the Orb with their expansive 'The Blue Room', were dallying with this idea, but it was far from in vogue. Still, *Melody Maker* were won over by such contrariness and hailed it as their Single of the Week. Verve supporters claimed the band were more akin to the new blissed-out indulgence of ambient music than overblown seventies rock dinosaurs.

The B-side, 'Feel', which was recorded on the lawn of the Manor Studios in Oxfordshire, was even longer, at well over ten minutes, and this tendency for protracted maundering was repeated on the UK tour to promote the single. In the reviews of these dates, sniping came in abundance, as this cutting, albeit rather funny, piece from Johnny Cigarettes in *NME* shows: '[Verve] have perfected the art of going nowhere slowly, creating druggy, mellow, sub-Spiritualized vibes punctuated by House of Love-flavoured floating guitar tickles and some hard MBV noise to stop you nodding off mid-song. Yes, it's shoe-gazing, only less exciting! Verve are basically bullshitting, muddling through with a collection of indie rock clichés. Every bloody lyric is "She's so high like a rainbow in my head" bollocks; every tune is a flat, featureless version of something mellow done seventeen times before: every guitar sound and every vocal utterance is predictable beyond endurance; and their influences hit you like a wet fish in the face. Verve don't make you happy or sad or angry, they don't make you want to go kill or shag or kiss or punch anyone. They just make you want to go to the bar.' John Mulvey, also in *NME,* was a little more concise, saying of Richard that he is 'a bit of a prat, if truth be known . . . who shimmies down the line between shaman and shitehawk most precariously'.

Undeterred by their first harsh reviews, Verve toured hard and partied harder. At London's famous rock 'n' roll Columbia Hotel, they invited a large gang of friends down from Wigan and proceeded to take over the bar, where the manager agreed to stay open after hours only if they bought him a drink in every round. They all got blind drunk, and the unconscious bar manager nearly got sacked. Despite only average reviews, the single reached Number 66 but many people felt this was a painful underachievement, and that a possible chart debut had been thrown away. The band, however, were not interested: 'We know we could have recorded a Top 40 single, but that wasn't how we felt at the time. We work on instinct and what comes out comes out. It has to be like that – it's the only honest way.' Richard also told the press at the time: 'People don't understand that there's bigger things than the charts. There's more at stake, if I can move a person emotionally, and take them to another place, it would mean more to me than being on *Top Of The Pops* or seeing us in the Top Ten. It's a big world out there and none of those things compare to touching someone with our music.'

This belief would cost Verve dearly in terms of commercial success in their early years. Their ideals were very admirable, but the combination of circuitous lyrics and music, their obsession with their own goals and ideas, and their lack of interest in the commercial arena, left the bosses at Virgin pulling their hair out in frustration. As for the hype that was growing around them, despite these chart failures, Richard was unconcerned, telling the press later that 'the odd time a band like us gets on the cover of the music papers, it definitely is worthwhile, there definitely is something there, and there's nothing around like that. There are so many times you get let down with bands that are hyped, and I'm not being arrogant and over-ambitious, but I don't think we were hyped enough. I don't think hype is the right word for us. I think truth is more like it.'

Although the band enjoyed the tour activities, Richard was already uneasy about the long-term implications of their impending success, as this extract from an interview in *Melody Maker* shows: 'The only thing that worries me about Verve is that touring will kill it, the thirst to play is not gonna be there. Because when we've got a gig in three weeks' time, I think about it every night and visualise what it's gonna be like and get really worked up about it. And I'm worried that playing repeatedly will taint that. It's difficult with something that's so free and unconstrained… ideally, I'd just like to play once every three weeks.'

*   *   *

Unfortunately, the demands of Verve's spiralling fame did not allow him this luxury. For the next single, 'Gravity Grave', released on 5 October 1992, the band set out on yet another tour. At least this time, with such a successful year already behind them, the band were preaching to the converted in many venues. *Melody Maker's* Ian Gittens said the band's live show was 'a holocaust, a sublime, supreme force of nature scorching all in their path. Richard Ashcroft was a preening, precocious, almost perfect STAR, the rolling, seductive blues-trip music was the ideal soundtrack for his self-adulation, and I stumbled away from the venue believing every word of their hype.' The single was another haunting epic, nearly nine minutes long, with one of the B-sides, 'Endless Life', even longer. Filled with bass warblings, largely indistinguishable lyrics ('My life is a boat, being blown by you' or 'The world just spins whilst mine stands still/Nothing's changed in your gravity grave'), indulgent guitar meanderings and very little else, the mantra-like song had the occasional chorus dotted across its length, and was effectively another case of commercial suicide. 'Endless Life' was even less specific, with virtually no tune at all, whilst the live versions of 'Man Called Sun' and the title track did little to bolster the release. Arguably the most interesting element of the single was the cover artwork, which showed a naked man standing at some water's edge, leaving behind him a beach strewn with his clothes, a microscope, some books and the stuttered letters 'v' 'e' 'r' 'v' 'e', oddly mixing Dali with Reginald Perrin. The beach where the band took the picture was Formby, near Southport, and the naked man was actually a friend of theirs identified only as 'B'.

'I told them they *were* making music six months ahead of their time. I didn't realise that it was more like *two* years. To be honest, I didn't expect people to get it.'

Perhaps predictably, the radio industry totally snubbed 'Gravity Grave', the press were only moderately impressed (save for a Verve fanatic at *Melody Maker*, who declared it 'another perilous flirtation with dissolution and the closer they get, the more beautiful they become'), and the single did not even puncture the Top 75, stalling well down at Number 196. *NME* concluded that 'there was a suspicion that Verve weren't so much making records as responding to their chemical intake and failing to reproduce in the studio the swooning peaks and troughs of their increasingly erratic live performances'. Even so, Hut's Dave Boyd remained philosophical, telling *Select*, 'When I heard "Gravity Grave" I told them they were making music six months ahead of their time. I didn't realise that it was more like two years. To be honest, I didn't expect people to get it.'

Proof of the inconsistency at gigs was highly evident during the tour for this single, perhaps mostly so at their home-coming show at Wigan Mill in the middle of October. The band were mediocre, and the pressure of playing to their hometown audience seemed to overwhelm them, with some observers enjoying the support DJs, Music of the Spheres, more than Verve themselves. Indeed, the highlight of the show was the fact that Verve walked on stage to David Essex's 'Rock On'.

At that Wigan Mill gig, *NME*'s Stuart Maconie had said, 'On tonight's form, the average Verve song live is too long, too dull and too lacking in ambition to aspire to the level that they clearly believe they are on.' Around this time, while Richard was busy telling everyone who would listen that they were the best band in the world, observers noted there was a potential gulf between his talent and that of his band. Without him, Verve were merely a good rock band, with him they had the potential to be brilliant. His charisma, his mouthy interviews, his stage persona, everything smacked of star quality, while all around him the rather more static band trotted out the numbers. Nick McCabe was clearly a gifted guitarist, but there was some unease about whether this alone would be enough. As *Melody Maker* put it, 'Do McCabe and Co. possess sufficient technical savvy to contrive the kind of zippy, snappy pop they're going to need to reach a larger audience and give Ashcroft the adoring following he deserves? Or are Verve doomed to languish on the margins, three musicians with credibility plus one exhibitionist without a public? We'll see.'

'mad richard'

'He's as mad as a carrot.'
melody maker

'If I won £18 million, I'd be dead in a week.'
richard ashcroft

While Verve already had the trappings of excess of many classic rock bands, there was an element of the media that increasingly focussed on the often bizarre utterings of Richard Ashcroft, a tendency which soon led to him being dubbed 'Mad Richard'. This nickname was supported by several aspects of both his character and live performance throughout 1992. At live shows, he was at times demented, clambering over speakers and dancing around in a peculiar, half-jumping, windmilling blur, interspersed with fixed, almost horrified stares through the crowd to the back of the hall. Other times he would suddenly flit up a speaker stack, touch the ceiling, then dash back down to smash the cymbals with his fists, and skim drumsticks across the stage before repeatedly screaming 'Come on!' off-mike at the guitarist or the crowd. He was like a hybrid of Mick Jagger and Bobby Gillespie, only much, much wilder.

This led to some observers inevitably suggesting that his fiery performance was not entirely without chemical assistance – and indeed sometimes it wasn't. However, Richard was clearly inextricably involved in the show itself: 'It's something that never enters my mind, I just get lost in it. It's like I'm on strings. It's like I'm washing myself. It's like I'm cleansing myself of all that crap that I've gone through . . . For twenty years I've been suppressed, and when you've had all these feelings suppressed for twenty years, and you're given a chance to show yourself, you want to explode.' Some observers laughed and claimed he was trying too hard, such as the writer who said he was 'narcissism made flesh, it's as if he's miming in front of a bedroom mirror, not performing in front of an actual audience'. Others recognised a man completely lost in his music.

'When you've had all these feelings suppressed for twenty years, and you're given a chance to show yourself, you want to explode.'

To the allegations of drug use, Richard could do little to deny this – in fact, he openly discussed it and its effect on his character. He talked in interviews of opening the right side of the brain through drug use, expanding the horizons of his muse and escaping the boundaries of reality that he felt could restrict the creative process. Clearly this idea was not entirely original, nor particularly revolutionary in the 1990s, but it appealed sufficiently to garner yet more headlines. 'It's not a classic case of getting wasted to write music,' he pointed out to Roger Morton in *NME*. 'It's not that sort of thing. For me, with the words, a lot of them seem to incorporate things like the sun and flying. It's something I was feeling all the time. I always wanted to fly. I always wanted to get away from where I was. Always wanted to feel warmer . . . you want to relate that to bigger things than chips and Co-ops and Tetley's Bitter. You want to relate to suns and flying.' What was often ignored in the headlines was his admission that drug use was only *one* aspect of his creative process, rather than the crucial element: 'It's not all of it. It's just another tool. I'd put travelling and seeing another country on a par with it. Because when it comes down to it, you still wake up the next morning and you're still in Wigan, and you're still looking out of the same window at the same view.' But despite such wider perspectives, Richard's espousal of drug use fuelled the Mad Richard myth throughout Verve's early career.

'I believe that you can do anything. I believe you can fly and I believe in astral travel because, if I thought I *was* just going to *walk* around this place for the next fifty years, I don't think I could exist.'

However, what really made the media flip about his oddball tendencies was his repeated discussion of his stepfather's Rosicrucian views, in particular his belief in astral travel, whereby a person can move outside of the confines of his own body. He first hinted at that when describing his feelings during a gig: 'When we play live, I've got a million thoughts swimming through my mind. And sometimes people mention Damon from Blur as a comparison and that really pisses me off. It trivialises my feelings. Because when we play, I feel like I'm flying. I'm obsessed with flying. And when we play live, it's the nearest thing to being lifted off this earth.' The core of all the Mad Richard accusations came during that same interview with Roger Morton of *NME*, when talk meandered around to his rather unorthodox beliefs. When asked if he believed he could fly, Richard responded: 'Yes. I believe that you can do anything. I believe you can fly and I believe in astral travel because, if I thought I was just going to walk around this place for the next fifty years, I don't think I could exist.'

Interviews with Richard at this time were never dull – he also said his stepfather could book them a gig at New York's Madison Square Gardens just by thinking about it. He talked of the potential to elevate people's bodies by mind patterns alone and the power of achievement by daydreaming. When ridiculed in *NME* for such eccentricity, he quietly retorted, 'I actually believe that I could fly if I put my mind to it but everyone's embarrassed to hear me say it. Why? Because everyone's

'When *we* play,
I feel like I'm flying.
I'm obsessed
with flying.
And *when we*
play live, it's the
nearest thing
to being lifted off
this earth.'

'So call me
Mad Richard
if you like.
In these times
I consider it a
compliment . . .'

*Ashcroft's performances sometimes
transcended rock 'n' roll, touching on
shamanism – a testament to his mystical
beliefs and the influence of his Rosicrucian
stepfather.*

embarrassed to think big. Everyone's scared of the unknown. Everyone's frightened when, for even a split second, they think about who the fucking hell they are and where they're going and what happened before they existed.'

Writers described his bedraggled looks as another example of increasing mental instability. Net curtain cravats often encased his spindly neck, his gaunt face fixing people with his jagged eyes, underlined with deep shadows from sleepless nights and too much of everything. His broad Lancashire accent and cascading ragged haircut made him seem like a parochial lunatic to city-wise journalists. 'He looks like . . . a vagabond poet, a psychotic dandy, a gay rag and bone man,' said one writer. All these factors made great, humorous copy at his expense, such as a column from *Melody Maker* entitled 'The Crazy World of Richard Ashcroft' in which they listed five points that proved he was completely bonkers. The list was: refusing to wear underpants, wearing the other band members' clothes, sleeping on Simon's floor, being thrown out of music class for playing the glockenspiel with chopsticks, and, oddly, having had some experience as a hairdresser, during which time his clients thought he was gay. It was also rumoured that he had lost his passport so many times that the authorities were considering investigating the possibility that he was selling them on. In return, Richard became a lunatic magnet himself, with increasing numbers of strange types approaching him at gigs in the vain hope of some degree of rapport with a similarly troubled mind – at one Scottish gig, a man walked up to him, stared him full in the eye and told him he would die young.

At first, Richard seemed not to mind this tag, but he began to tire of it as it came to dominate interviews. Initially, he was glad that it separated him and Verve from what he saw as a mire of indie no-hopers. As he told *NME*, 'If I'm called Mad Richard just because I get involved in a gig, because I lose myself, how banal and boring does that make everything else? What's the crime? Surely music was invented so that we could experience something sensational and something strange, something that takes us out of our everyday existence. So call me Mad Richard if you like. In these times I consider it a compliment . . .' However, the appeal dwindled as the mad tag became something of a millstone. He later explained that he may have been misunderstood (although this is wishful thinking perhaps): 'When I said I was expecting to fly, I was just trying to explain what we do as a band, to explain that we can do anything and we're gonna go as far as possible.' When he realised the 'mad' label threatened to dwarf the band's musical output, he became really agitated, telling *Vox,* 'The "Mad Richard" thing, that was really orchestrated to . . . divert things. It was very demeaning, very . . . English, probably the fucking Tories. And we knew we were one of the most important bands in the world from when we started. A lot of journalists should not be in a position to even write about it. Everyone can have their opinion, but when it becomes personal towards me, when it doesn't even try to explain what the fucking music sounds like, that used to piss us off big-time.'

*   *   *

Before moving to Sawmill Studios to record their debut album, Verve supported the Black Crowes for two late-November 1992 dates at Brixton Academy. After a fairly indifferent year of playing average live shows to Verve fans, the band were now faced with playing to audiences who had never heard of them. They rose to the challenge and produced some of their best gigs to date. Along the way, Richard picked up the habit, from the Crowes' lead singer Chris Robinson, of playing barefoot on a rug placed across the stage. In addition to this, he would enter the stage with coat and shoes on, take them off ceremoniously and then start to sing (Bernard Butler later did exactly the same when Suede played the Brit Awards). 'I don't like to think too much about it,' Richard later told *NME,* 'otherwise it would all become too self-conscious. But I guess it's like a shedding of the skin y'know? You take off your skin, abandon yourself, enjoy it, share this experience, and then you put the skin back on again and you're off.'

In charge of recording the debut album was John Leckie, who had been in the audience at the band's second London show at the Camden Falcon (although he was actually there to see the headliners, Whirlpool). One of the most famous producers in the world, Leckie had initially started as an engineer at Abbey Road Studios, before working with Pink Floyd, the Fall, Simple Minds, Ride, XTC and Radiohead. He would also be at the helm for much of the protracted Monmouth Studios sessions for the Stone Roses' painfully delayed, and ultimately ill-fated, second album, *The Second Coming.* Leckie, who himself enjoyed a reputation for alleged drug habits, was highly curious about Verve's music. What he saw that night at the Falcon had an immediate and lasting impact on him, as he told *Q* magazine: 'I just knew they were special. For days after, I kept thinking about this band and checking the music list to see when they were playing again. They're the only band I've ever approached to work with. What really impressed me was the dynamics, how devastatingly loud they could be, and how quiet and sensitive they could be. At points you could hear a pin drop – and then it would just explode.'

Up until now, Verve had displayed an almost pathological fear of the recording studio's potential to sterilise a song that they knew worked brilliantly live. Their hopes for the debut long player was that it would capture the energy that they possessed at gigs. With this in mind, they came to the studio almost completely unprepared, with just two songs loosely formed, and nothing else, encouraged by an unrestricted brief from their record label. 'It's a very loose arrangement which will probably make the producer have a nervous breakdown,' warned Richard, but Leckie was more than happy to work with them in this fashion – he later said that his relationship with them was 'almost telepathic'.

'*What* really impressed me *was* the dynamics, how devastatingly loud they could be, and how quiet and sensitive they could be. At points you could hear a pin drop – and then it *would* just explode.'

Experimentation was the key, and many songs' final takes were recordings of lengthy improvised marathons – Richard claimed that over 80 per cent of the album was thought of during informal jams. The finished album was almost a recording of works in progress, as Nick explained to *Lime Lizard*, 'That's one of the good things about us, because it's a living breathing thing. You can see some bands every night, and it's just cold. I think some people see quality as being professional and tight, but what does it matter? I like seeing a band fuck up one night, and then seeing them excel the next.' With Leckie's own open attitude, drugs were in evidence at the sessions, although they were not the driving force:

'It varies, some nights it's enhanced, some nights it's not. If drugs are there to be used and take it further, they will be, and if they're not, the natural feeling of music is as high as I've ever been. When the band is all working together . . . there's no drug that compares to it.' Having said that, Simon later admitted, 'On our first album, we were just taking ounces and ounces of hash. All I remember about that part of my life is living in a fucking haze.'

One evening at the studio, Richard and Sobbo vanished for most of the night, raising fears for their safety, only to turn up the next morning having paddled a fibreglass canoe down a nearby river, armed only with a paddle and a large bottle of Jack Daniels. Richard found the whole recording experience a strange one: 'When it was all going on, I was in a corner of the room, looking down and sort of laughing at myself. It's such a surreal setting you can't help but get a kick out of being involved with it. It's like being involved in this ridiculous movie.' He also revealed his principles for the sessions, saying, 'Anyone can pick up a guitar and play "Heroin" by the Velvet Underground, but not everyone who picks up a guitar can create something that sounds fresh and new. What's the point of closing yourself in when you've been given the chance to make music? Maybe you'll make only one record in your life, that's the way we see it when we record. We record as if it's the last thing we're ever going to do, purely because you get the most out of yourselves.'

Before the album could be released, Verve had another single to put out, namely 'Blue', which saw the light of day on 10 May 1993. At around the three-minute mark, this single was their most commercially primed release yet, and with Leckie's guiding hand and not inconsiderable airplay, there was genuine feeling that chart success was imminent. The track itself was perhaps their most poppy outing also, briefly telling the tale of two 'would-be drugstore cowboys stealing a car and getting into trouble' (it was later used in a film about a serial killer, who played the song every time he murdered someone). The B-sides were more par for the course, with longer, more sauntering trips such as the harmonica-led 'Twilight', the wistful 'Where The Geese Go', and the storming 'No Come Down'. But despite all the odds for once being stacked in Verve's favour, this single also stalled well outside the Top 40, at Number 69. Perhaps it was the lyrics, with Richard's tendency to err into pretentious waffle, which *Melody Maker*'s Ian Gittins summed up as 'bogawful Pseuds' Corner lines like "I am the crease in the shirt that this world wears."'

a definite article

'Verve will be the biggest group in the world. It's only reasonable that we should be playing in front of 40,000 people. Minimum. When we play those little gigs now, I see some bloke kind of looking on indifferently, I think, "Just wait. In two years time, you'll be boasting about how you saw Verve in a little club and you were freaking out down at the front." History has a place for us. It may take three albums but we will be there.'
richard ashcroft

'I don't think we're ever gonna achieve what we wanna achieve. It would be impossible, but that's the point. To aim further. But I think, for our age and experience, we've made a fucking great first album and established a great place to start.'
richard ashcroft

On 21 June 1993, Verve released their debut album, *A Storm In Heaven*. Surrounded by Suede's rejuvenated London-centric Bowie-isms, Blur's defining *Modern Life Is Rubbish* tirade, and the mainstream successes of grunge, the album sat uncomfortably among its contemporaries. Verve's opening volley of effects-laden singles had offered the public almost formless songs swathed in cloaks of noise, and this album followed a similar path with only a smattering of traditional tracks, most notably perhaps 'Slide Away' and the single 'Blue'. The remainder, both lyrically and musically, were shapeless without being aimless, with the band's spacey backdrop proving at last a worthy sound for Richard's impressive and at times other-worldly, yet still melodic vocals.

From the opening blast of distortion to the closing wild fade-out, the 40 minutes of kaleidoscopic music made for an impressive, albeit patchy debut. Brian Cannon, the band's resident artwork designer, had provided a fascinating sleeve – the themes of birth, youth, middle age and old age, portrayed through images of Thor's cave in Staffordshire, a burning car pictured in Billinge, a cellar in Upholland and an old man wearing Richard's clothes in Birkdale cemetery.

The opening 'Star Sail' was dreamy and feedback-tinged, setting the tone for the huge, cavernous psychedelia to follow, complete with squalling guitars and white noise (it was later chosen for inclusion on the soundtrack to the titillating but dreadful Sharon Stone film *Sliver*). Richard's troubled mind is immediately apparent with the lines 'Hello it's me, it's me/Calling out I can see you/Hello it's me, crying out, crying out/ Are you there?' Next up was the hypnotic 'Slide Away', a popular song in their gigs, and here it gelled nicely on record, displaying the range of dynamics between beautiful quiet and raging noise that had so attracted John Leckie to the project. The first real signs of the influences on them arise with the blatantly Led Zep-inspired 'Already There' (where Richard reiterates his stepfather's theories with the lines 'You can do anything you want to/All you've got to do is try'), but then the swirling and compelling 'Beautiful Mind', another live favourite, brought Verve firmly back into 1993. The graceful power of 'The Sun, The Sea' with its rather poor lyrics – 'It's myself I feel/She calls me calls me the sun the sea yeah' was then followed by the flute-led 'Virtual World', where Richard's vocal performance peaks, with raw yet impassioned cries over the spaced-out, shuffling beat. Indeed, throughout this album, Leckie seemed to have drawn a new level out of Richard's vocals, giving him an abrasive touch that was often desperately needed amongst Verve's more self-indulgent ramblings.

The rather disappointing and lyrically bloated 'Make It 'Til Monday' and nondescript 'See You In The Next One' slowed the momentum down somewhat, but the excellent single 'Blue' raised the stakes yet again. The most specifically lyrical track on the album, the free-form jazz blow-out of 'Butterfly', talked of chaos theory, and the random effect single events might have on the world – 'You could flap your wings a thousand miles away/Butterfly/A laughing salesman sings/His world so far away.' Elsewhere Richard's words were largely indistinct. 'Butterfly' also contained Nick McCabe's best moment on the album, with a threatening riff and subtle texture that reinforced his fast-developing reputation as one of Britain's most creative guitarists.

'We like all sorts of music, but it doesn't mean you have to hone in and rip it off. Because our music tastes are so wide and so varied, we're not in love with one particular band. You sponge in all those things, and then in turn you don't rip them off, because you've got so much going on there in your head.'

On its release, Verve were predictably very confident of what *A Storm In Heaven* represented, and were far from shy about informing the media of how brilliant they were. In *Lime Lizard*, Richard said, 'Maybe with the new LP, and a few records that have proceeded it, the doors are finally being broken down as far as expression on record, and expression as far as the band are concerned. The way I look at it is that it's time for people who want to create to create, and people who want to be out there in mediocrity to sink.' He also proudly boasted, 'The problem with a lot of bands is that if I like the Byrds – and okay, I like the Byrds, we all like the Byrds – it doesn't mean we have to pick up Rickenbackers and sound exactly like them. We like Funkadelic, and we like touches of Led Zeppelin, we like all sorts of music, but it doesn't mean you have to hone in and rip it off. Because our music tastes are so wide and so varied, we're not in love with one particular band. You sponge in all those things, and then in turn you don't rip them off, because you've got so much going on there in your head.'

Some observers found this apparent boast of originality a little unrealistic. After all, traces of many bands were clearly evident on the record, including Led Zeppelin, Can, Funkadelic, My Bloody Valentine, the Doors and even Echo and the Bunnymen. Whether you agreed with Richard's claims that Verve were fusing these with their own original sound was largely a matter of opinion, but in an environment where Suede's Brett Anderson was openly aping Bowie and Bryan Ferry, and where Blur were about to open the floodgates of the sixties' plundering that would fuel Britpop, he was right not to feel tainted. As for criticisms that the record was overly dark, Richard made no excuses for his thematic focus, telling *Melody Maker,* 'We've always been a dark band, dark in a way that can be quite frightening. A lot of people heard the first takes of the album and said, "You're obsessed with death." Maybe I am. I think you're a fool if it's not in your mind. My father died when I was eleven. If I died the same age as my dad, I'd only have eighteen years left. That's terrifying. So that gives you an urgency.'

'*We*'ve always been a dark band, dark in a *way* that can be quite frightening. A lot of people heard the first takes of the album and said, "You're obsessed with death."'

The media response to *A Storm In Heaven* was pretty strong. *Melody Maker* hailed it as a great new work, but, with rather more realism, the *3rd Degree* said, 'The album is impressive because the whole group have stuck to the thoroughly uncommercial guns of their earlier work and released a rock record which is hugely out of synchronisation with these fake-hedonistic, star-fucking times.' Elsewhere, *Alternative Press* were ecstatic, with reporter Dave Seagal saying, 'I've just spent an intense week listening to *A Storm In Heaven* . . . and I can barely contain my excitement. Not since 1988, when My Bloody Valentine's *Isn't Anything* busted open rock and loosed a new alien magma, have I been so all-fired intoxicated by a piece of music. Unless something extraordinary happens, *A Storm In Heaven* will be the best album of 1993.' Much later *Rolling*

The classic line-up of The Verve (left to right): Nick McCabe, Pete Salisbury, Richard Ashcroft, Simon Jones.

Stone was to describe the album as 'a majestic affair, a modern-rock mosaic soaked in languorous swaths of 1990s psychedelia that recalled in places the Rolling Stones at their most woozy and Velvet Underground at their most velvet'.

There were also several poor reviews, including a piece in the *Sunday Times* which complained that 'if you texture and torture the sound to this degree, you begin to convey the impression that you don't believe in the songs; and while there are some rather flimsy wails here, there are also some more robust rockers which don't benefit from carrying this much sonic baggage'. Thinking of the media hype that had surrounded Verve throughout 1992, *Q* magazine was equally reserved, saying, 'Ultimately, their undoing may be that their fame rests entirely upon journalistic whim rather than any groundswell of popular support.' Overall, however, *A Storm In Heaven* was justifiably well received in the press.

Despite the good reviews and the band's own lofty predictions, *A Storm In Heaven* only reached Number 27 in the UK album charts, a severe disappointment to all involved. The sombre air was continued when they performed before Jamiroquai at Glastonbury later in June, having to borrow instruments as their own gear had been stolen from their van. To make matters worse, as the band started their set, live on Radio 1's festival broadcast, Nick's amp loudly, and to much embarrassment, blew up. A spate of gigs following this were later cancelled when Richard suffered a throat infection and Nick came down with a painful kidney infection. Also, by now the band were a little more downbeat about the album, with John Leckie revealing their concerns in *Select*: 'We were searching for things, and waiting for it to rain down on us. We came close but neither they nor I thought they managed it. It lacked the overwhelming effect of the Verve experience, maybe as there was no audience to feed off.'

However, there would certainly be an audience to feed off on the forthcoming tour to promote the album. Part of the tour was in America on the Lollapolooza bill, the travelling festival of high-profile alternative acts that had been instigated by former Jane's Addiction main-man Perry Farrell. In recent years, the bill had seen bands like Nirvana and Pearl Jam playing alongside Ice Cube and Ice T, and a series of British acts had enjoyed prestigious slots, including Primal Scream and the Jesus and Mary Chain. This time, however, Verve were the only British act on the bill, but that did not stop them enjoying the experience. Next up were some European dates supporting Smashing Pumpkins, before they flew back to England for their own headline album tour in the autumn. Perhaps tellingly, Verve's tour manager declined on their behalf the chance to support the Pumpkins' gigs in Amsterdam, for fear of the band 'losing it big style' in the red light capital of Europe. Verve got on very well with the Pumpkins, and James Iha even bought Richard a blouse with a butterfly design when he was in Cambridge. On the business side, this period also saw the departure of Dave Halliwell, the long-time friend who had managed the band from the start, but who now decided to step aside and let more established people take the reins. The band were sorry to lose him, as he had been instrumental in their progress, but were glad to welcome new manager John Best, who was a partner in their press agency. Halliwell meanwhile went on to look after Verve's merchandise and manage the Beta Band.

'We were searching for things, and waiting for it to rain down on us. We came close but neither they nor I thought they managed it. It lacked the overwhelming effect of the Verve experience, maybe as there was no audience to feed off.'

In the midst of all this, on 20 September, the band released their next single, 'Slide Away'. With the A-side taken from the album, the record also contained acoustic versions of 'Make It 'Til Monday' and 'Virtual World' which were entertaining enough, and it was generally well received. Despite the single failing to puncture the Top 40, its warm reception primed the situation nicely for the forthcoming UK tour. In support of them were a Manchester quintet newly signed to Creation Records, who were being hailed by label boss Alan McGhee as the next Beatles – Oasis. At this stage, all Verve knew of this band was a demo whose four tracks would soon become as much a part of the modern pop lexicon as the Gallagher Brothers themselves – songs like 'Live Forever' and 'Columbia'. As soon as the two bands met up, they bonded instantly, with Richard and Noel Gallagher becoming particularly close friends. Throughout the tour, as Oasis's reputation began to build, Richard always watched their entire set from the audience. Here, at last, was a band he could identify with. He said to *Q*, 'When they were playing "Live Forever", there were two people sat on the floor and there was me on the balcony . . . Real moments. Real fucking moments. And that's why whatever happens, I'll know them and they'll know me forever because it was beyond bullshit, before fame, before money, before anything.' He called them his 'soul brothers', who came from 'a proper music-loving background'. The gigs were fantastically good. Even when things did not go so well, the atmosphere was buoyant – after a power-cut in Glasgow, Richard, Noel and Nick performed an impromptu a cappella version of 'She'll Be Coming Round The Mountain', with Bonehead on spoons! Various alternative rock stars were seen in attendance at gigs, including ex-Smith Johnny Marr, and there were frequently dozens of media types and journalists present. At the London show, the bands were rumoured to have kept the guest list executives outside all evening out of spite, though they denied this.

One fairly major blemish on this otherwise enjoyable period was the news that Verve's choice of name might be the subject of legal action from a jazz label, a Deutsche Grammophon/Polygram subsidiary with American offices of the same title. That label alleged that the potential consumer confusion between the two (i.e. German jazz fusion record company and English psychedelic blissed-out drug-addled rock stars!), might have detrimental effects on their all-important profits. Despite questioning this supposition, the law was not on the band's side. The record label Verve demanded that the band either undertake extremely expensive market research to prove that no commercial conflict existed, or alternatively pay a fine of £25,000 and change their name. The band pondered the possibility of calling themselves Verv, if for no other reason than for the chance of releasing an album called *Dropping An E For America*. Unfortunately, common sense prevailed, and by the spring of the next year, the decision had officially been taken and Verve became 'The Verve'.

1994 saw The Verve writing and rehearsing preliminary material for their second album, and then a spate of their own European headline dates in the New Year, during which they aired some of the new material, including 'Black And Blue' and 'Mover'. A German TV appearance was followed by a scheduled appearance at Glastonbury again. Unfortunately, after the previous year's poor show, things were even worse this time – the band had to cancel completely after drummer Pete broke his ankle. Despite The Verve's rock 'n' roll reputation, the accident was caused by nothing more sinister than a glass of water. He got up at home in the middle of the night to get one, but having just moved into the house with Simon, he was unfamiliar with the layout in the dark, and consequently walked into a picture frame that was leaning up against a wall. It smashed down onto his ankle, breaking it. In hospital, doctors put him in a plaster that would require a minimum of ten weeks to repair the damage. He ended up leaving the metal pins they inserted in his foot in place permanently. In the light of this, a gig at the Clapham Grand in London was cancelled, as was Glastonbury, as well as all the scheduled US dates that were designed as a warm-up to yet more Stateside Lollapolooza gigs in the summer.

Before they arrived in America for the salvaged Lollapolooza shows themselves, The Verve released an import album in the States on the Virgin US subsidiary Vernon Yard, entitled *No Come Down*, which contained B-sides, out-takes of various sessions and alternative versions of previously released tracks. It was the first appearance of 'The Verve' on record, and contained much self-indulgent jamming and improvisation. There was also a ten-minute live recording of the tour favourite 'Gravity Grave' from Glastonbury 1993, early singles and acoustic versions of 'Make It 'Til Monday' and 'Butterfly' as well. It was far from a 'greatest hits'-style package, but worked well in educating the American market about the band in preparation for the tour. This time, The Verve were there for all six weeks of Lollapolooza. Unfortunately, by the end of the jaunt, they had very nearly imploded.

getting on *with* the gallaghers

'America freaks me out. New York brings out the best in me.
It brings out the devil in me.'
richard ashcroft

'It was every day of the past six years catching up with me.
Still, time of our lives, this.'
richard ashcroft

Things initially seemed to be going well. The Lollapolooza dates were in front of huge crowds, regularly over 30,000 people, and, being the only British band on the bill, The Verve attracted much attention. And away from a series of good live shows, the band had an increasingly demanding round of promotional obligations, including requests to play retail conventions, various embarrassing radio interviews, live acoustic sessions, and so-called 'walk-throughs', whereby they literally walked through large record stores shaking the hands of the bewildered staff in a vain attempt to get them to know their product better.

However, The Verve's extra-curricular activities nearly proved their downfall. Rumour has it that inordinate amounts of alcohol and other substances were being consumed by the tour party, and with friends travelling over from Wigan, the excess was accelerating. When added to their exhausting schedules, crap American television and sleepless nights of cramped travelling, the signs were not good. Then, on 11 July, after playing Kansas City's Sandstone Amphitheater in Bonner Springs, a blind drunk Sobbo lost his rag and smashed up his room at the West Inn Crown Center Hotel, hurling over $450 worth of furniture out of his fifteenth floor window in the process. He was promptly arrested and frog-marched to the local police station, along with the roadie who had joined in the drunken spree. Meanwhile, Nick and Simon were quietly enjoying a drink in the downstairs bar when they were determinedly befriended by a drug dealer and phone sex-line operator, who insisted on them getting legless with him at his flat round the corner. Before they left, they hardly noticed as Sobbo was marched past them, flanked by hotel security and police.

The next day, the band played their gig and afterwards a particularly pale and gaunt-looking Richard immediately complained of feeling ill. Earlier in the tour he had been befriended by a sixteen-stone Hell's Angel who kept insisting that Richard looked exactly like a young Keith Richards. In true 'Keef' style, Richard had been drinking very heavily for several days, and was barely eating. Backstage, he began to shake uncontrollably and had to sit down, with sweat pouring off his forehead. Then he started convulsing. The band gave him drinks of water and held ice on his head, but it melted on contact. They panicked and called an ambulance, but because of the size of the venue and the crowd, it took over half an hour to arrive, by which time Richard was in an even worse state. Simon later admitted that he thought the singer was going to die. Richard was rushed to hospital where paramedics discovered he was was severely dehydrated, and missing seven pints of fluid from his system. 'It was an extension of Richard not thinking about just the basic human things,' manager John Best recalled in *Select*. 'You know, like putting food in your body and occasionally having a glass of water when it's 110 degrees and you've drunk God knows how much alcohol the night before.' Back on the stage, Kim Deal of the Breeders anounces 'Did you see Verve? You'd better go see them quick, before they all die!'

The next day, with Sobbo fresh out of jail, and despite doctor's orders to rest, Richard performed a quiet and restrained show. When he neared the photographers' pit down the front, they snapped away quickly, having noticed the marks on his arms from where the saline drips had been removed only a few hours previously. The rest of the shows after his collapse suffered – the usually highly supportive *Melody Maker* held no truck with the shoddy performances they witnessed: 'The Verve are a collective crap Jesus. It makes us embarrassed to be British. They're so fake, so transparent, so lacking in substance . . .'

'When I *was* in the ambulance, I remember putting my thumb up, taking the piss. There's a scene in *The Simpsons* when the stunt rider guy does his jump over the shark pool, puts his thumb up and then he falls in.'

When questioned about his near-fatal collapse, Richard was remarkably dry about the experience, telling *Q,* 'When I was in the ambulance, I remember putting my thumb up, taking the piss. There's a scene in *The Simpsons* when the stunt rider guy does his jump over the shark pool, puts his thumb up and then he falls in. It was like, "Yeah, kids, Evel Knievel's alright." Funny. But funny and scary 'cause I thought I was gonna die. I had some mad doctor holding me cock while I was trying to pee in a bottle and two drips coming out of me arms . . . I know now I'm really lucky I didn't die.' Asked whether this would temper his future excess, he replied, 'To a certain point, yeah. I don't wanna go there again. It doesn't make you wary, really, it just makes you realise that when you're young, you don't know how far you can take it until you realise your limits . . . your physical and mental limits.' He also admitted that 'America nearly killed us'.

In retrospect, it was surprising that The Verve had not suffered such an implosion before. The rigours of touring America have destroyed many bands, and their own lack of a sense of self-preservation placed them in a particularly vulnerable position. Richard admitted as much a few months after the debacle, when he told *Guitar Magazine,* 'No wonder we went a bit mad on Lollapolooza. If you could get us a room full of instruments, a PA and a bit of draw, then we'd be in there jamming . . . Instead you wake up in a car park outside some superbowl stadium 25 miles from anywhere, where there's nothing to do but drink. It would get to anyone, that.' He also said in *Melody Maker*, 'If you're taking the lifestyle you have at home away as well, that's gonna lead to madness. [And] because we're 24-hour party people . . . you've got to keep it going because if the morale drops, the gigs suffer. You can't take time off . . . but for someone to get that pissed up and pissed off in the middle of America to start that craziness, that's how mad it gets.'

On the band's return to England, their live show did not improve – a tepid show at Reading Festival was warmly received, but this was more because of the band's profile than the actual gig itself. The Verve were burnt out, they needed to recover. But far from this happening, things were about to take a turn for the worse.

*   *   *

'There was something in the stars around that time, it was a turning point in everyone's lives, people growing up, changing. Plus they were taking a lot of E. It was a recipe for emotional shutdown.'
dave boyd on the sessions for *a northern soul*

Returning from the US dates, The Verve set up to record their second album in a shabby industrial warehouse near Wigan, which Richard called 'a black room, a claustrophobic pit'. Having been rootless for so long, they craved a return to their hometown. They had heard a story on tour about Keith Richards, and how when the Stones had been touring America one time, Dean Martin had publicly ridiculed them. Richard identified with that and said it inspired them for the next album: 'That's what happened to us . . . we just thought, "Fuck you all, we're gonna delve into our black hole in Wigan and make the greatest music you've heard in your life."' The idea was to record much of the album there, largely performing live takes. However, this did not prove practical, despite the help of piles of 'industrial-strength speed'. What the band hadn't taken into account was that they were still emotionally and physically exhausted from their US rigours. That, added to the atmosphere in the studio, created a

Opposite: As The Verve's 1994 Lollapolooza dates degenerated into destructive chaos, drummer Pete 'Sobbo' Salisbury was arrested for trashing his hotel room.

rollercoaster of excess that no-one could control. By starting in the ultra-reality of Wigan they had inadvertently worsened the situation, as Simon explained to *Melody Maker*: 'When you come home after you've been through all the madness, that was difficult to deal with. You're drained by America, then you come back to this "real" environment. That's supposed to be your life, but you don't know who you are. You don't know whether you're the person you were on tour or the person back at home.'

Abandoning the initial plan, they decamped to Loco Studios in Wales, where Owen Morris, the producer of Oasis's debut album *Definitely Maybe,* was to steer the project. He had been invited to the rehearsals and took little time accepting the offer to produce – 'they just blew my head off'. The Verve were similarly bowled over by his very raw and visceral production ethos for that Oasis record, before which he had been a virtual unknown.

'That's *what* happened to us . . . *we* just thought, "Fuck you all, *we*'re gonna delve into our black hole in *Wigan* and make the greatest music you've heard in *your* life."'

Simon was determined to avoid the mistakes they had made with their debut album, as he explained in *Exclaim!* magazine: 'We had all of two songs written and walked in and made the rest of it up. I mean, we fucking deserve a medal, because it was the hardest thing I've ever done in me life, to go and do a record when you have two songs. So I was like, "I'm not going through that again. We are writing these songs before we even step through the doors." As an artist makes better paintings, we're getting better at making songs. We're just gifted. I don't wanna blow me own trumpet, but we're pretty damn gifted people.' Having said that, although they had some songs formed, they had no real preconceived idea of the overall feel of the album – that would be left to their muse.

Initially things went well and rough takes were recorded quickly and with good results. However, as the sessions lengthened, things started to turn sour. Vast quantities of Ecstasy were being consumed by the band, and alcohol was flowing. The search for the muse meant that night after night would be spent driving aimlessly around waiting for something to happen. Other times they would wait for their inspiration just sitting in the studio getting stoned. Or they would put Can or Funkadelic on the stereo at full volume and dream about being as good. Other times they would be more proactive, beginning jams that would go on for hour after hour, in the vain hope of something finally gelling. While taking colossal amounts of drugs, they often deprived themselves of any other sustenance, including food and sleep. There was one three-week spell where they survived almost entirely on Ecstasy alone. 'There's an aim and a cause when we jam,' Richard later told *NME*. 'We do it for hours at a time: build the intensity and then drop it down to tease people, to tease ourselves. We're great teasers. it's like prolonging the orgasm. People buy cream for that but we've got music . . .'

On the odd occasion when this worked, it was a great experience, but more often than not it stalled and the tension within the studio grew. Even when a take was apparently in the bag, the band would trash it, saying they needed more. 'We're perfectionists,' Richard later explained. 'We have to deal with the pressure of listening to the greats, as opposed to listening to Echobelly. We set ourselves a very tall order. It was hard.' The studio bills were growing and the album was nowhere near being finished, but Richard rather pretentiously refused to budge, telling *NME,* 'It was all about waiting for the inspiration. Feel was everything. And if it wasn't there, we'd get really, really depressed. The song'd sound good but there wasn't that magic. We were waiting for the magic all the time: like, "Where is the magic, man? We need it!"'

At one point, when they were recording a track called 'History', Owen is reported to have ended up in tears of frustration. Later, in despair at the weeks of meandering, he allegedly hurled a chair at the studio glass partition, leaving a large bullet-sized hole in the pane. He was said by Richard to have then demolished a pair of monitor speakers as well. Richard admired the producer, saying, 'he's such a geezer for coming on that voyage with us'.

In the midst of all this, wild stories of The Verve's madness were filtering out into the media. The drugs, the drink, the tension and the isolation of the rural studio meant they had long since lost track of reality. At one stage, the band wanted to smash a £100,000 tape machine to pieces just to create an interesting sound to finish the album off.

One night a studio worker refused to let them in, so concerned was he for the safety of his equipment. Richard later said, 'When we were recording *Northern Soul* we went into the scary zone, to places where it takes a long time to come to terms with what went on there . . .'

While the rest of the band seemed to revel in this chaos, Nick was struggling. His girlfriend was pregnant but the relationship was quite unstable. To make matters worse, he often clashed with Owen in the studio. To further complicate things, he developed something of a paranoia, and no amount of praise or confidence boosts would ease his concerns. Although he and Owen had their cross moments, the producer in fact had only good things to say about him. In *Guitar Magazine*, he hailed him as 'without a shadow of a doubt the most gifted musician I've ever worked with. I haven't a clue where his genius comes from, but at the same time he's a complete and utter nightmare. He'll never play the same thing twice. Now, you can ask Noel Gallagher to play the same guitar line a hundred times, and as long as there's a good reason for him doing it, he'll do it. But with Nick you've got no chance. But that's what he does, y'know?' Despite all this, Nick still came away with fond memories of some of the sessions: 'We just went in and played . . . and that's when you know you're playing really well, when you don't have to think about it. There were three weeks during the making of that record which I'd have to say were the best I've ever had in my life.'

In the middle of all this, Richard went completely off the rails. His own relationship with his girlfriend of six years, Sarah, had finished (there were rumours she had left him for a mutual friend), and he was devastated. At a severely low ebb, he vanished on one occasion for five days straight without anyone knowing his whereabouts. Then a two-month spell of contemplation saw him draw even closer to the edge. He tried but failed to work things out with his girlfriend, and that sent him even lower. In the meantime, he was 'uncontactable' for weeks on end, unavailable for press duties, and totally skint – he even took to dodging train and bus fares and scamming off hotel bars. These apparent swathes of calm were interspersed with outrageous behaviour – one story has it that he took a hire car and drove it round and round in circles on a manicured lawn, so much that one of the rear wheels eventually fell off.

Looking back over this dark period, Richard acknowledges the depths he fell to, telling *Q,* 'It was a period of extremes, and I suppose the tail end of that was my lowest point. Lowest point mentally. The psychosis, I've had it all. I've seen visions come out from nowhere, I've been Syd Barrett, lying in my sleeping bag in the recording studio. And I'm glad I've been there, really. At the time, it frightens the life out of you because once you lose that control over your thought processes to that extent, you're fucked, man. But if you're caning anything, you're gonna get to the point where the demons come and I was seeing the fucking demons.'

'If love is a drug/Then I don't need it.'

Amazingly, when Richard rejoined his fellow band members, many of the lyrics and ideas he had swimming around his confused head matched the musical landscapes they had come up with. So eventually, over a long time, the album gradually began to solidify. When it was finally complete (after some orchestral work at Abbey Road Studios), Owen Morris looked back on those days and said in *Guitar Magazine,* 'They don't really need a producer, because they will do a producer's head in. They did my head in, completely and utterly. There you go. That's life. It's a fantastic album at the end of the day, but it's not a process that I'd ever want to go through again.' Richard, still the confident optimist despite everything that the traumatic last few months had seen him go through, managed to draw some inspiration from the tumult: 'It felt like I'd been through a huge emotional storm. But I got something out of it. Out of all the torment, I had a diamond. And that's what great groups survive on.'

*   *   *

Before the second album could be released, The Verve put out two singles, 'This Is Music' and 'On Your Own'. The first came out on the first day of May 1995, and, for Nick at least, it was an unusual song. For the lead guitar line, he used a cast aluminium guitar from the early eighties which only had three strings and was completely out of tune. Still, the finished article was an excellent comeback – after all, The Verve had not released a single for eighteen months. With the opening line 'I stand accused, just like you/For being born without a silver spoon', it was an oddly political piece for The Verve, with Richard's vocals more snarling and vicious than ever before. Elsewhere, his lyrics seemed more controlled, with lines such as 'If love is a drug/Then I don't need it' and the ambiguous reference to his drug theories in the words 'There's a door in my mind that's open wide/Come inside, come inside.' The dope smoke and hippy mantras seemed to have been overtaken by shorter haircuts and harder-edged songs. The musical backdrop was supercharged, much rockier, and placed The Verve closer to Oasis and the Stone Roses than the psychedelia of their earlier career.

'I don't resent the upper-classes, but they take the piss. I remember when Chuck D first came over to England, every one of our papers had something about Princess Di's new haircut. And he's coming from a neighbourhood where kids are gettin' shot on the corner. I mean, I love England. But, when you analyse it, it's totally fucked.'

All the same, Richard was anxious not to be suddenly portrayed as a political, campaigning band – he had already been burnt by press generalisations: 'It annoys me what people think of us,' he told *Melody Maker* angrily, 'All that hippy narcissistic shit. All that came about 'cos we emerged at a time of self-love, Suede 'n' all that, and that image was something journalists put on to us. We've never been hippies.' Despite his downplaying of the political content, the cover artwork for 'This Is Music' displayed a man in the Headingley district of Leeds with a sandwich board, displaying the song's opening line in a distinctly preacher-ish style. Moreover, Richard described how he wrote 'This Is Music' after meeting a man who had studied at Eton, having been shaken by the head start this person had in life. Although he says the song is about a character, he admitted that it just as easily could have been him. 'I don't resent the upper-classes, but they take the piss. I remember when Chuck D first came over to England, every one of our papers had something about Princess Di's new haircut. And he's coming from a neighbourhood where kids are gettin' shot on the corner. I mean, I love England. But, when you analyse it, it's totally fucked. We've had dickheads in power for so long. The eighties were a terrible, greedy decade. The wrong people making ridiculous amounts of money.' At the same time, he denied the value of the protest song, saying it had been 'bastardised too much over the years'.

The comeback single was generally well received, but there were still a few snipers out there who reserved venom for the Wigan band, such as *Melody Maker*'s Cathi Unsworth, who said, 'Mad Richard stands at the top of a cliff, arms outstretched. All around him, The Verve's music resounds with the overblown grandeur of the wild and desolate landscape that surrounds him. Jump, you fucker, jump.' The public did not agree, and gave The Verve another Top 40 single, with 'This Is Music' reaching Number 35.

Since the recording of the album, Nick's girlfriend had had her child, but the two had become estranged. During the pregnancy, Nick had played Steve Reich records close to the womb, and when born, his baby, Eleanor, would always stop in her tracks when she heard that music. Simon Jones had married his American girlfriend, Myra, on Valentine's Day and Richard had started dating Kate Radley from the band Spiritualized, after her relationship with that band's Jason Pierce had finished. So, by the time The Verve came to play their first gig of 1995 at London's Raw Club in June, things had changed considerably. Unfortunately, it was a very lacklustre performance, but this did not stop the general sense of anticipation that was building around the second album's impending release.

Next up was the single 'On Your Own', on 12 June. A much mellower song than its predecessor, the wandering track was more of the old Verve, but still contained enough of Richard's compelling vocals to shine through. Again, his lyrics were developing, with lines such as 'Life seems so obscene until it's over,' and the sad aching lament of 'All I want is someone who can fill the hole.' Some observers felt it was an odd choice of single, decidedly uncommercial at such an important career point with the next album pending – the seven-minute tedium of B-side 'Dance On Your Bones' raised a few worried eyebrows again, and 'I See The Door' was also generally disappointing. Fortunately, The Verve's choice proved correct this time, as it gave them their biggest hit to date, with the single reaching Number 28.

'Dance On Your Bones' appeared to be about heroin, and this raised a spectre that had been hovering around Richard Ashcroft for some time – that he was hopelessly lost in heroin addiction. He said the song was about 'about the Devil sweeping you up into all kinds of depravity', and he admitted that he had experience of the drug. But he said this was only vicariously through friends who used it, and he denied having taken it himself. At the same time, he was unsurprised and largely unperturbed by the media's hunger for such gossip: 'Let them say what they want,' he nonchalantly told *Vox*, 'rumours go around me anyway, I think because I'm quite a private person, we don't play the scene, never have done, so people will never truly get it. And that's the way I want it. I don't want people to understand it . . . Every fucker seems to be coming back with a distress story, and with us there's no distress any more.'

Just in case Richard might think things were going too well, two instances of bad luck hit him just before the album release. Firstly, he lost his home – he had returned from some Verve dates to find his flat in Wigan locked up, and all his possessions sold by the landlord, in lieu of £3,000 he owed him in unpaid rent. Richard was largely unconcerned by this fairly major hitch – it is rumoured that when he was told the news he shrugged his shoulders and said, 'Possessions, so what?' He simply gathered up in a plastic bag whatever belongings he had left and slept on friends' floors for months – 'I just wanted to get back in touch with life again.'

Then, while supporting Oasis at the Bataclan in Paris (the Mancunian band had by now catapulted to tabloid ruling-the-world status), Nick lost his backstage pass and got into an argument with a security guard. The guard responded by hurling him down a flight of stone stairs, breaking his finger in the process. This meant cancelling yet more dates, including a high-profile support slot with Oasis in Sheffield. Nick couldn't play for a month, but seemed chirpy enough, saying, 'If the doctor had only left one finger free, I could have put a slide on it.'

* * *

Much has been made of the connection between The Verve and Oasis. After supporting The Verve on tour, Oasis's career went supernova, and

Opposite: Liam Gallagher of Oasis, giants of modern mainstream rock and champions of their friends The Verve.

within eighteen months they were one of the biggest bands in the world, with the antics of the Gallagher brothers plastered across tabloids the world over. Since they had met before each band were famous, the friendship was unfettered by the politics of celebrity, and they consequently had many wild nights out together. One heavily publicised incident occurred during August 1994, while they were both in Sweden for the Hultsfred Pop Festival. During the day, the hotel management made the crucial mistake of leaving a teenage girl in charge of the bar facilities, and the drinks cabinet was emptied of its supplies in a matter of a few hours. Noel and Richard then trashed their hotel room completely, an incident which in itself made the front pages of the local papers. Their notoriety grew much more however, when, having been ejected from their disgusted hotel in the middle of the night and in search of more alcohol, they fruitlessly tried to break into a nearby church to guzzle down the

'A bunch of space cadets, led by Captain Rock. They're all bonkers.'

communion wine. The authorities reacted in horror and threatened to ban both of them from Sweden for life.

Richard clearly related to Noel in particular, talking of Oasis's creative synergy and calling them 'kindred spirits', while Noel famously called The Verve 'a bunch of space cadets, led by Captain Rock. They're all bonkers.' The compliments went further than that, with Oasis borrowing the song title from The Verve's 'Slide Away' for their debut album, and Richard penning the lyrics to 'A Northern Soul' after Noel's famous US tour walk-out. Perhaps the most celebrated example of these two bands' close relationship is the Oasis track 'Cast No Shadow', found on the record-breaking second album, (*What's The Story) Morning Glory?* Dedicated to Richard, the song is a beautiful ballad about a man who is 'bound with all the weight of all the words he tried to say', and 'as he faced the sun he cast no shadow'.

Richard found out about this track just before he went on stage at London's Astoria, when Brian Cannon, the band's sleeve designer (and Oasis's as well), played him a demo. Richard's reaction was to tell the

Scotsman, 'I don't know what I thought. I mean, it's a big deal to people because it's on a huge Oasis album but I think Noel would have done it even if they were selling 400 copies. It's something between me and Noel. It touched me, simple as that, because it is a beautiful song and at the time it was quite relevant to me. Oasis are honest. They make soul music. It's coming from Noel and the band's hearts.' It has also been reported that Richard thought that in the song Noel was suggesting he was a vampire!

The media has often wrongly insinuated that without Oasis's championing of The Verve, the Wigan band would not be where they are today, but that is unfair, and Richard is right to dismiss such accusations. Indeed, he has made as many 'we are the best band in the world' proclamations as Noel, and probably did so first. 'What would Noel expect me to say? No, we're not as good as Oasis?' In actual fact, the two bands are polar opposites in many ways, with Noel's working-class hero stance set against Richard's escapist, astral theories, and Liam's yob image in contrast to the Mad Richard persona. That said, the two have obviously forged an invaluable and close friendship. Not close enough for Noel to concede too much ground however, as shown by him calling The Verve 'the second best band in Britain'.

splitting up is easy to do

'I don't care what's gone before this band. There's too many bands engrossed with what other bands think and do, and I don't live like that. This is a totally personal thing . . . it's all coming from inside.'
richard ashcroft

While The Verve had been on sabbatical, Britpop had taken the music world by storm. After a period of several years languishing in the shadow of American music's success, led by the world-conquering feats of Nirvana and a host of grunge supporting acts such as Pearl Jam, Hole and Soundgarden, British music had begun to fight back. With the charts having been filled for some time with tiresome re-issues and one-hit wonders, it was time for genuinely new talent to break through. After the briefly popular, speed-fuelled success in the music press of the so-called 'new wave of new wave', led by punk throwbacks like S*M*A*S*H, the tide began to turn towards more substantial new music.

In 1992, *Melody Maker* had hailed Suede as 'The Best New Band In Britain' on what became a famous front cover, and many observers credit this band, led by the enigmatic, Bowie-mad Brett Anderson, as paving the way for Britpop's creation. Brett's London-centric lyrics and foppish

English sexuality flew in the face of the American/Seattle scene, which was quickly becoming as corporate, macho and overblown as everything it had originally stood against. Suede's eponymously titled, Number 1 award-winning debut album sharply turned attention back towards the UK's own rich heritage for the first time in years.

At this point, The Verve were hailed as the big rivals to Suede – but the latter's more succinct and commercial music meant that Richard's band soon fell by the wayside in the chart races, although they continued to hog the music press.

One band who did keep up with Suede was Blur, led by the irony-drenched lyricism of heartthrob Damon Albarn. Their re-invention for their second album, *Modern Life Is Rubbish*, and their distinctly anti-American stance made them perfect contenders for refuelling British music. Their classic third album, *Parklife*, seemed to launch Britpop into the commercial stratosphere with its massive sales and frenzied tabloid attention. But the Britpop honours were then, of course, taken by the latecomers, The Verve's close friends Oasis. They released their first single at the same time as Blur's second album, but within months they had grown into the most talked about British band for years.

The fiery Gallagher brothers enjoyed a love–hate relationship with the tabloids, and their antics rocketed the band to global success, particularly with the record-breaking sales of their second album, (*What's The Story*) *Morning Glory?* In the process, the concept of the so-called 'new lad' was invented, along with the Lad Bible, *Loaded* magazine, which became an instant best-seller on the back of its 'birds, booze and bonking' editorial content.

Britpop's ranks were swelled by a host of quality bands, and also hordes of lesser acts – Supergrass, Pulp, the Boo Radleys, Shed Seven, Portishead, the Bluetones, Marion, Powder, Dodgy, and the fleetingly fashionable but soon-to-be-forgotten Sleeper. Older artists enjoyed Indian summers to their careers, with the likes of the Modfather, Paul Weller, and Shaun Ryder both regaining previously failing popularity. Also, many sixties and seventies bands who were name-dropped by the new elite – groups like the Kinks, Steve Harley And Cockney Rebel, and, of course, the Beatles – all enjoyed unexpected and often very generous surges in back catalogue sales. The repercussions of Britpop went further than that – fashion, tourism and the entertainment industry in general blossomed, and as grunge lost its figurehead when Kurt Cobain committed suicide in April 1994, Britpop took over the music world (at least in the UK). Record sales rocketed by 14 per cent in 1994 alone, grossing an all-time high of £1.5 billion.

It was a rich new seam of British talent, but The Verve had absolutely nothing to do with it. They were absent for most of 1994, burning out in America or suffering the hideous recording experience of *A Northern Soul*. Musically and visually, Britpop was a million miles from anything they represented, even with the rockier comeback single 'This Is Music'. Although they had been heavily involved with Oasis, the nearest they came to Britpop was one night when Richard visited Liam's house and got out of his car to be sprung on by dozens of photographers, who duly moaned with disappointment and put their cameras away when they did not recognise him. With the release of *A Northern Soul*, Britpop was at its zenith, with a much-publicised chart showdown between Oasis's 'Roll With It' and Blur's 'Country House', which even made the *Six O'Clock News*, but The Verve continued unaffected. For them, Britpop was something that happened to other people.

* * *

'Our ambitions have always been really grandiose and ridiculous, but that's the way I like it. My ambition is to make some classic records and do some incredible tours and I wanna be someone.'

richard ashcroft

'If you open up musically or lyrically you're gonna be prone to people taking it to the extreme. I think the more I do it, the more I'll be gettin' to the point where someone's gonna blow me head off in New York. It's always there.'

richard ashcroft

On 3 July 1995, as Britpop peaked, The Verve released their second album, *A Northern Soul*. Nine of the twelve songs ran to well past the five-minute mark, and the record was full of their trademark swirling guitars, huge rock themes and meandering, sprawling songs. Yet it was much more powerful than previous material, richer in lyrical thought and musical texture, and easily their most accomplished project to date. With the swathes of strings and ethereal guitar work, it was also a much classier record. They had actually recorded twice as many songs as they needed, but were not happy with half of them, and vowed to return to them at a later date.

After the opening musings of 'A New Decade', the album's first classic track, 'This Is Music', hit home. The clumsy title belied the majestic wanderings of the song, but the song was strong enough to support it, despite its having suffered because of the substandard B-sides on its single release. The pained and gentle 'On Your Own' followed, which left a disturbingly uneasy feeling about the ultimate solitude of life.

The title track, allegedly written about Noel Gallagher's vanishing act on Oasis's American tour in 1994, was a brilliant monster. The highlights of the album were its rockier tracks, and this was no exception, with Richard singing of the yearning to find a place to live: 'This is the tale of a northern soul/Looking to find his way back home . . . I was born in a rented room/My mother didn't get no flowers.' The character in the song was clearly very dear to Richard, and he reacted angrily to comparisons with Pearl Jam's troubled lead singer, Eddie Vedder, telling *NME,* 'The character who's singing that song is way more messed up than Eddie Vedder's ever been. But at the end of the song he looks around and says, "I'm too busy staying alive. Too busy living." There's got to be a blue horizon. There's got to be hope. We've been given too much angst-ridden shit from America for too long. I'm sick of hearing these upper middle-class white boys whining about shit I can't relate to. Just sick.'

After the average rock of 'Brainstorm Interlude' and the gentle ripple of 'Drive You Home', the next classic track arrives – 'History'. Written about the end of his six-year-long relationship, this song is perhaps the most lyrically direct Richard had ever been. (Coincidentally, Spiritualized's revered 'Ladies And Gentlemen We Are Floating In Space,' was about the heartbreak caused by the split between Kate and Spiritualized's Jason Pierce, after which she started dating Richard.) A tremendously beautiful ballad, like 'On Your Own', it confirmed him as one of the best songwriters of his generation. 'Relationship-wise, I'd had an easy life up to that point,' he admitted, but the break-up of that love affair hit him hard: 'I've gotta tell you my tale/Of how I loved and how I failed,' he sang.

Opposite: Simon Jones, bass guitarist. The disintegration of the band's original line-up followed hard on the heels of their album A Northern Soul.

With handclaps courtesy of Liam Gallagher (who, with Noel, had frequently visited the album recording sessions – Richard later returned the complement with backing vocals on the album *Be Here Now*), the epic track was perhaps the album's strongest song. Apparently, Noel was so impressed when he first heard this track that all he could say was 'Fuck me. Bastards!' The staggering vocals and bitter lyrics portray the betrayal Richard must have felt deeply. 'It's just written by someone who's sat down and thought about things. Who's gone through the classic stage of a few weeks gettin' pissed up and goin' down to those pits, listening to Big Star at six in the morning. I think . . . I hadn't given up on love.'

The indifferent 'No Knock On My Door' is followed by the guitar mastery of 'Life's An Ocean'. Ironically, despite much of The Verve's apparent spiritual and mystical imagery, much of this album was actually rooted in quite mundane issues: 'Imagine the future/I woke up with a scream/I was buying some feelings with a vending machine.' With regard to this excellent track, Richard explained to *Melody Maker* that it was 'a Stanley Kubrick vision of the future. This guy has got soul but he's being suffocated by commercialism. Products. And he's stood in the middle of all this madness . . . The song's just a future shock guy at the end of his emotional tether.' The record closes with 'Stormy Clouds, Stormy Clouds (Reprise)', bringing to a completion a fantastic, challenging, emotional spell of music.

Perhaps the album's biggest achievement was Richard's approach to lyrics and vocals. Whereas previously he was liable to lose his thematical path in escapism, now and for the first time, he addressed many of his concerns and thoughts directly. He told *Alternative Press* why this change had come about: 'It was a very big escape from when we first formed the group. Now it's a kind of melting pot for overt emotions, which makes recording sometimes scary and a lot of times exhilarating. When someone's singing straight to the point about what's going on, if the guy means every word, people are gonna connect with it and it will become more accessible.'

Lyrically, he had been inspired by the poems of the late-eighteenth and early-nineteenth century visionary William Blake, in particular his *Songs Of Innocence And Experience*. This had also led him to Aldous Huxley, a big admirer of Blake. Indeed, several actual lines from Blake's poem 'London' found their way in to the track 'History', inspired by the time he was wandering around the capital trying to get his head around the split from his girlfriend. Elsewhere he recognises his band's success on 'New Decade': 'The radio plays the sounds we made/And everything seems to feel just right.' He admits his obsession with music on 'This Is Music', saying, 'Well music is my life/And loved by me.' The repetitive 'Lies' repeats the idea of an emotional void, pleading 'I've got to get rid of this hole inside,' while 'So It Goes' includes what became known as a classic 'Richard Ashcroft-ism', the depressing albeit realistic philosophy of 'You come in on your own in this life/You know you leave on your own', strangely mixed with semi-comic couplets such as 'I'm just a poor little wifeless fella/Another drink and I won't miss her.' The cathartic nature of much of the album appeared to have given him new hope: 'I know I'll meet someone else and things will change. I do need someone else to stabilise me. Like "This Is Music" says, "I've been on the shelf too long."'

He continued, unusually eager to discuss his motivations: 'Lyrically the whole album is me asking myself, "Who the fuck am I? Am I the guy in 'This Is Music', standing tall in the world with these huge guitars around him like the king of rock 'n' roll, or am I the guy in 'A Northern Soul' who's wasted and desperate, or am I the guy in 'On Your Own', who's in between life and death, or am I the guy in 'Life's An Ocean' imagining the future and buying feelings from a vending machine, am I this future shock guy?" But I'm all of them, you see. It's dangerous to fracture your personality too much, but that's what it was.'

The stunning cover artwork was created in a warehouse near Tower Bridge, London, by projecting a sixteen-metre image of the band onto a huge wall, just as Sobbo walked in through a door. For the band, this represented the depth and dimension that the music represented at this time. The inner images of the band, taken during that near-fatal American tour revealed just how ravaged they had become, with all of them looking exhausted and mad-eyed. All the same, prior to the album's release, The Verve were in typical cocky form, with the usually quiet Sobbo saying, 'it's one of the best albums in the last ten or fifteen years. As good as Nirvana's or the Roses.' Nick said, 'This album contains some of the best music I have ever heard,' whilst Richard, not to be outdone, proclaimed, 'We know it's a special record. It's not throwaway, it's got soul, it's come from us and what we've been through. We will be put up there with the Stone Roses and other greats.'

He pre-empted the release with a side-swipe at the current Britpop fashion, saying, 'I don't think we can afford to pay too much attention to what's going on at the moment . . . I can't listen to the radio or watch music on television. It's just impossible.' When it was released, *A Northern Soul* entered the UK album charts at Number 13, and was widely acclaimed by the critics, despite its discord with that year's fashions. A previously reserved *Q* magazine said, 'The Verve are suddenly the definite article,' while *Melody Maker* boldly said, 'it is the brashest, boldest, most adventurous, fucked up and human album of the year.' *NME* were a little more reserved, but displayed a cunning sense of foresight when they said, 'Global domination? Maybe next time, chaps. Maybe next time…' Oddly enough, in one of the many features in the media to promote the new record, Richard dropped a hint about one of the new songs he had already written for the third record, saying, 'It goes "the drugs don't work, they just make me worse, and I know I'll see your face again". That's how I'm feeling at the moment. They make me worse, man. But I still take 'em . . .'

* * *

After another indifferent Glastonbury performance when Nick's amp blew up yet again (Richard continued on his own with a tambourine while the amp was repaired), The Verve set off to the States on a tour that would also encompass the UK. Before they flew out, Richard married Kate Radley, five years his senior, in secret on 11 July 1995, in Stroud. They kept this quiet for another two years, with Richard continuing to refer to the life of a single man in any press interviews. At first, the enthusiasm for the forthcoming album tour seemed considerable, but pretty soon cracks would begin to appear that were far, far more serious than any outside observer could possibly have imagined.

Richard pre-empted the new dates with a volley of excitable quotes about how much he was looking forward to touring, especially in America, despite the near-terminal experience he had the last time he played across the Atlantic. In the light of the traumatic previous year or so, many friends worried for his mental and physical health in the midst of another mammoth jaunt. Richard, for his part, seemed undeterred:

Opposite: Live dates in 1995 veered from the peak of intensity to uninspired sloppiness, mirroring the instability which resulted in The Verve's first split.

'It's gonna be an experience singing these lyrics. If I'm true to myself and believe in what I do then I can't fake it, I'm going to have to get into it completely. And, to get into it, I've got to go through it all again.' At the same time, he expressed some concern: 'If I'm still stuck in this rut a while from now, I'll be really messed up. I wonder if I'll be able to sing these songs every night on tour. I have to feel the songs when we play. I don't know if I can re-live the last six months for another year.'

Despite having played only a few gigs in 1995, The Verve sounded great on tour and reviews were strong, although after their return to Britain their show at the Phoenix Festival was lacklustre. However, just seven weeks into the tour, after a fairly sorry show at Glasgow's T In The Park festival on Sunday 6 August, the shock news filtered through that The Verve had split up. The show at Strathclyde Park itself was a seedy, disappointing affair, almost like watching The Verve come apart at the

'The *Verve* hypnotise the audience with their laid-back but epic rock. Dramatic, swirling chords pulsate as singer Richard Ashcroft prowls the stage, acting every part the rock god.'

seams. Richard was clearly physically unwell, stumbling around the stage, pent up with frustration and apparent disdain for his band colleagues. He was in a bemused state and eventually lost his cool completely, punching the drummer and throwing cymbals across the stage. Despite this, some reviewers still thought everything was okay, such as the writer from the *Observer*, who said, 'The Verve hypnotise the audience with their laid-back but epic rock. Dramatic, swirling chords pulsate as singer Richard Ashcroft prowls the stage, acting every part the rock god.' *NME* were a little less enthusiastic: 'The Verve . . . are now dragging out the sublime "Gravity Grave" to such ludicrous week-long extremes it could almost fill a Roger Dean-designed triple-LP bastard concept package on its own.'

The band's manager John Best broke the shock news to the media and he later said, 'Richard is very tempestuous and I think that has a lot to do with his sense of conviction. He couldn't fake it if he didn't feel it.' All that the stunned fans were left with was The Verve's swansong, the aptly named, elegiac 'History', released on 18 September. The posthumous single faired well and reached Number 24 in the UK charts but, callously, the media seemed to have suddenly turned on a band that was once their darlings. The previously enthusiastic *Melody Maker* now proved to be the band's sternest critics – their single review simply stated, 'Last and also least . . . it's official, the final single from The Verve. They are history. Pleased? Me too.' The *Strathclyde Telegraph* were no more charitable, saying, 'Hands up those who like The Verve, what's that, about three, no maybe four or even five. To be honest, The Verve were the most overrated thing since Christianity. Both are based on men with long straggly hair and both will never come back.'

While Britpop had raged, more popular than ever, The Verve had slipped into oblivion. Defeated by their own sense of grandeur, their overambition, and their distaste for the commerciality of their art, maybe they were doomed to failure. At least they had tried. The final sickener was the artwork for the 'History' single. The idea was to reflect the song's theme about the broken relationship between Richard and Sarah. Again, designed by Brian Cannon, it contained pictures of the band in Times Square, New York. In one version of the CD package, they stood near a sign saying 'Life Is Not A Rehearsal'. On the main CD artwork they stood under a cinema sign displaying the words 'All Farewells Should Be Sudden'.

apart, alone

'I wish it hadn't happened this way, but he's only 23,
and he'll do something amazing again.'
the *verve's* manager, john best, commenting on the split

'I had a lot of stuff to sort out, I was in a mess . . . I've benefited most out of
this, really, 'cos I've got a sense of whatever goes wrong doesn't really matter,
'cos I fell to the bottom and it wasn't so bad.'
nick mccabe

Many observers were amazed the band had taken a nosedive at such a crucial point in their career. *A Northern Soul* had sold more copies in its first month of release than its predecessor *A Storm In Heaven* had shifted in two years. With huge tours scheduled for America, Europe, Japan and yet more high-profile support slots with Oasis, the general consensus was that The Verve could be on the verge of international success.

The immediate post-mortem into the split revealed the extent of the internal divisions that had rent the band apart. At the centre of the split was, of course, Richard Ashcroft. It was widely known in the industry that, despite the success of *A Northern Soul*, Richard had returned from their final sell-out tour of America with more than just physical problems.

He was suffering from a severe viral illness, had been boozing again, and had a much worse recurrence of debilitating polyps in his neck that he had previously suffered on an earlier tour. Some said he had never fully recovered from the insanity of the recording sessions for *A Northern Soul*. Others said he was completely underwhelmed by the rousing reception his band had been given in the USA, and that this made him question his motivations for writing music. The Verve had, after all, started when he was just nineteen, and so many things had changed since then without him or any of the band being able to take stock of those developments. Practically, the band had been growing apart for some time – whereas they had all originally come from the same area of Wigan, as they grew up and formed relationships, got married and had children, they were unavoidably pushed away, both geographically and emotionally, from each other.

Confidants suggested Richard take a year out to recover mentally and physically, but he refused. He admitted he might not have been in the best state of mind to make such a monumental decision, but insisted he had made the right choice by splitting The Verve up. He strenuously denied there were any musical differences, saying, 'We needed some breathing space, I just didn't know quite how things were going to work out. We weren't communicating at all: things just weren't going to plan . . . I'm The Verve's biggest fan, y'know . . . the point is, we had to split. I couldn't lie any more. I don't like living a lie and we had to do it.'

In the face of scurrilous (although sadly inevitable) rumours that hard drug use was at the core of the split, Richard was indignant: 'Let me tell you this, there are things that have gone on in The Verve that I won't be talking about . . . until the day I die. If we were an American band I might talk about them and go on to sell fifteen million albums on the back of it, but because we're from Wigan, and we all love each other, we're not gonna start talking about it. I know some people get their catharsis through interviews, but not us. Let's just say there was a cloud over us . . .'

Although he was the one who had broken the band up, it was almost as if Richard was still shocked by The Verve's demise. He decamped to Cornwall, where he holed up in a cheap hotel overlooking some cliffs. While he was there, sitting on the bed listening to the radio, dwelling on recent events, a DJ on BBC Radio 1 said, 'The Verve are history and this is their final single, "History".' Richard was devastated: 'I was more choked than I've ever been in my life. The total is always more than the sum of the parts and when I heard that blasting out I was gutted. I was sure that if we'd toured after "History" we'd have taken off.' The band's last ever interview was also published at this time, in which the writer called The Verve 'the most important band in Britain, and potentially the most thrilling group of the nineties'. Later that week, Richard's mother rang and told him that 'History' had charted – he cried down the phone and his depression deepened.

He acknowledged that even he was not in control of the situation, revealing to Jo Whiley on BBC Radio 1: 'I didn't mean it, you know, it's not something I wanted, it's not something I went out for. It's something that was almost beyond my control, do you know what I mean? I felt devastated, really, and I knew it was gonna be a long time before we could be back together and there was gonna be a lot of turns and twists along the way to get us there, but that's the way it is you know, you have to . . . you have to go down . . . these roads to get to where you should be really.'

Meanwhile, while Richard cut himself off, the rumour mongers had a field day. He was allegedly a heroin addict, he was sleeping rough, and worst and most ludicrously of all, he had planned a suicide pact with Sobbo and Simon. All complete rubbish of course, but in his, and the band's, absence, these allegations circled around The Verve's corpse.

While not sleeping rough, he did continue to sleep on friend's floors and even back at his mother's for a while, before finally getting a flat with Kate, his wife, in Bath. Pretty soon, however, he was talking of new material, new bands and new ideas. To many people's surprise, only three weeks after the split, he had teamed up again with Sobbo and Simon, and also recruited old schoolfriend Simon Tong for keyboard duties. Immediately, people cast aspersions about Nick. At the time, all three other members were reported to be 'extremely unhappy about the band's demise', but clearly it was a more one-sided split than was first imagined. 'When Richard left,' his manager John Best revealed in *Q*, 'it was unclear what was going on really. He just sort of said, "I'm out of here, I'm off." And then over a period of days or weeks, it became clear that Simon was going and Peter was going and it was kind of like, "Everyone who's not leaving the band, put your hand up now." Suddenly Nick was the only one who hadn't actually left.'

The only thing that was sure at this stage was that the new band would not be called The Verve – despite their obvious differences, Richard recognised that without Nick the band could never be that. Although he was in Bath and the other three were living in London, they started to rehearse new material – if nothing else, the traumatic recent weeks had given Richard plenty of material and inspiration.

Meanwhile, things were not working so well for Nick McCabe. When the band split, he moved back to Wigan and signed on the dole. By the time of the split, he and Richard were hardly talking to each other, so to insiders it was not surprising that the singer started up again so soon without him. Nick meanwhile sank further. Towards the end of the band, he had been terribly unhappy. 'We had a joke,' he told *NME*, 'about me being the kitty litter tray. Any shit that happened to anybody I absorbed it. I'm in the corner freaking out . . . And I couldn't really appreciate it. That's how I used to think . . . To a lot of people I seem like I'm insane.' This downward trend affected the band atmosphere badly: 'It was just personal. The band's always been completely solid but it got to the point that all I had in common with the rest of them was the music. If I sat down for five minutes, I had a lot of stuff weighing on my head. I didn't feel comfortable anywhere. My home life was a disaster. And because I came back to the band with a miserable attitude, I didn't bring much joy to them.'

He did enjoy being around his daughter Ellie, but he had not succeeded in mending his relationship with her mother, and that took its toll. He later theorised that this was at the core of the desperate depressions of his that had plagued the final days of The Verve. In the aftermath of the split, he was so demoralised that he virtually abandoned his musical career altogether, save for a few electronic doodles that he taped for his own pleasure, in what he called a 'diary form'.

Unfortunately, Nick's mental health worsened. Ironically, while most people felt that Richard, with his 'mad' persona and difficult childhood, would be the one to suffer the most emotional distress, it was the quiet, reserved and apparently ultra-normal guitarist who was actually the one who struggled most to keep afloat. He temporarily tried to join a new band, but 'couldn't be arsed with the hassle'. Thereafter, he did very little for an entire year. He had always been short of social skills but now, adrift without a musical focus, he was spiralling out of control. His depression was such that over the Christmas of 1995 a friend tried to have him sectioned for his own safety. He had hit rock bottom. 'It had to happen really. I knew it was coming. I had a lot of stuff to sort out, I was in a mess. Stuff happening in my personal life. I had a kid and all that went a bit strange.'

Meanwhile, the other former members of The Verve were starting to rehearse new material. Richard in particular had found the recent rollercoaster of emotions incredibly productive, and there were no signs that his search for perfection had been tempered by his experiences. One industry tale relates how he played a bunch of new songs to a close friend on his acoustic guitar and asked him what he thought. When that friend said they were good, Richard pestered the listener for confirmation, finally asking him if they were the best songs he had ever heard in his life. The friend said, 'No'. Richard duly binned all the songs and started again from scratch. Tapes of his new songs, labelled simply 'Richard Ashcroft', began circulating the industry, and there was very quickly much excitement about them. The first rumblings of a solo career seemed to be taking shape.

John Leckie was one of the first to hear these songs, and he immediately got in touch with Richard and suggested they meet up, just to lay some rough versions of these tracks down. In the end, the other three joined him, and over two months of sporadic recording they completed a demo of 32 songs, with almost another twenty substantial ideas on top. Among them were s'Bitter Sweet Symphony', 'The Drugs Don't Work', 'Sonnet', 'One Day' and 'Space And Time' (other tracks recorded finally surfaced as B-sides, while others remained unaired – 'Misty Morning Dew', 'Don't Blame It On The Father', 'Come On People', 'Song For The Lovers', 'A Little Bit Of Love', 'Jerusalem', 'Monte Carlo', and 'New York'). Although Leckie felt it was Richard's best work yet, the singer knew something was missing – a dynamic lead guitarist.

Richard's friend Noel Gallagher had been watching all this with growing concern, worried that his mate would never make it back to the music scene. In order to try and resuscitate his self-belief, Noel offered Richard a solo acoustic slot supporting Oasis at their forthcoming gig at New York's Madison Square Garden on 14 March 1996. So, after all these years, the gig that Richard had said he could visualise and make happen (a statement for which he was derided heavily) was finally going to take place. Armed only with his acoustic guitar, Richard sat in front of the massive Manhattan crowd and played a beautiful set, including 'The Drugs Don't Work', 'Sonnet' and 'Space And Time'. However, despite the warm applause, and the relief he felt at playing live again, Richard knew the gig had served only a limited purpose: 'It charged the batteries,' he told *NME*, 'but it was never going to be anything more . . . It was lonely as well. I ain't a solo artist. It was mad, really.' Rumours that he would then make solo acoustic appearances at Oasis's gigantic Loch Lomond and Knebworth gigs proved unfounded.

Further rumours swelled the speculation about Richard's future. A Dutch magazine reported that Noel Gallagher had said Richard's new band would be called Sensation, and that the songs were 'very, very, very good'. *Select* announced (with their tongue firmly planted in their cheek) that he had in fact joined a Rolling Stones cover band called Rockery, which had already signed a deal with the tiny Windmill record label (within hours the Internet was rife with gossip about this!). He also shot a cover feature for the trendy London fashion magazine *Dazed And Confused,* and even signed a modelling contract with top label Moschino. Some observers wondered if he would ever fully return to the musical fray.

Richard was happy with the Leckie demos, but wanted something more, so he called up Owen Morris, who had worked with him so well during the Bachannalian *Northern Soul* sessions. Richard felt his no-frills approach might be the key, but after only two weeks at Rockfield Studios in Wales, it was clear that the jigsaw was still incomplete. No tapes at all were compiled during these sessions.

Richard continued to address the absence of a lead guitarist. Bernard Butler, formerly of Suede, and latterly a hired-gun guitarist along the lines of ex-Smith Johnny Marr, seemed an interesting option, particularly as he had publicly declared himself a huge Verve fan. The two met up at Bernard's house and rehearsed once, which Richard initially felt was quite productive, but after dwelling on the experience for two weeks, he decided it wouldn't work after all. 'I said to him at the end of it, "Look, you've got your own thing to do, I've got my own thing to do and there ain't space for it."' Richard later told *Q*, 'Sometimes certain chemistry works and sometimes it doesn't, and in that case it didn't. But I left with only total respect for the geezer. He'd been in a band with people who he didn't communicate with whatsoever and he was off on his own battles.' Richard

Opposite: The 1995 split left guitarist Nick McCabe alone and isolated, facing psychological problems which built up during his time in The Verve.

also blamed the fact that 'there were too many egos'. Bernard simply said 'there was nothing in the air'.

Next up was another of his generation's great guitarists, ex-Stone Roses John Squire, after the two met by chance at a party hosted by Eddie Izzard (ironically, at a time when rumours were flying around that Nick McCabe might become Squire's replacement in the Stone Roses). Their drunken plans for a collaboration never really got off the ground: 'All I said to John was: "Listen, man, I'm not on about forming a band here. Let's get in a room, if we only have it for ourselves. Let's make a tape and see what happens." But he went off on his gig and that was fine, 'cause I never really wanted to have a band with him. I just thought, "Wouldn't it be a real laugh if we just had a jam?"' That 'gig' Squire went off on was the Seahorses and Richard was again left with no lead guitarist (all Squire had to say about the brief liaison was that he was utterly bewildered by Richard's intensity).

'Youth claimed he *veered* Richard 'away from *wearing* old influences like the Roses on his sleeve and *towards* a more universal, classic approach.'

Frustrated by the failure to resolve his guitarist dilemma, Richard determined to continue, lest he lose momentum. Through his manager John Best, he was put in touch with Youth, the former Killing Joke bassist who has worked as a producer for U2, Polly Harvey, Nick Cave and the Orb. During the middle of 1996, the two met up at the Olympic Studios in Barnes, south-west London. For his part, Youth was not a great Verve fan but liked 'their big, visionary picture'. He brought a discipline to the recordings that Richard and the other three had never known – they turned up like office commuters at 10 a.m. and worked until the early evening, when they went home for a good night's sleep. Excess was cut to an absolute minimum. In addition, Youth claimed he veered Richard 'away from wearing old influences like the Roses on his sleeve and towards a more universal, classic approach'. With the help of the affable and exceptionally talented engineer Chris Potter, who had once worked with the Rolling Stones, the project started to gather momentum.

A good indication of this is the classic 'Bitter Sweet Symphony'.

So frustrated was Richard by the lack of progress with the new songs that he had at one time considered abandoning this track altogether. Youth was appalled at the idea and demanded they rework it, hailing it immediately as a landmark record. To complete the transformation, a new manager in the shape of former Wham! and Yazz aide Jazz Summers, supremo at Big Life Records, was enlisted. He revealed that 'when I heard "The Drugs Don't Work" I stood there with a lump in my throat,' Summers told the press. 'At times like that you know why you're in the music business.' The band liked his maverick reputation, and his powerful contacts in America seduced them after the relatively disappointing sales of *A Northern Soul* in the States. Things were starting to look very strong indeed. Richard, at this stage, still had no name for his new band, but he had an idea of what their debut album would be called – *Urban Hymns.*

coming together

'Emotionally, me and Nick needed a bit of space between each other. But I got to the point when nothing other than The Verve was gonna do for me.'
richard ashcroft

'I'd wanted to kill him on sight, although I probably would have shit myself had I seen him. So he called, and I said, "Y'know, I should tell you to fuck off, but it's my first love."'
nick mccabe

There was still one piece missing from Richard's jigsaw, and as 1997 dawned he finally acknowledged what it was – Nick McCabe. Whereas he had blamed the split squarely on his 'instinct', Richard now said that the same impulse was telling him to get back in touch with Nick, even though they hadn't exchanged a single word since the break-up of the band. 'When you get the inner voice calling you,' he told *NME*, 'you can deny it for a while but when it starts eating at your insides you have to answer it, you have to heed its advice, because that's your instinct and your instinct is the truth. In anything in life, a relationship or whatever, don't deny your instinct.' So, only one week into 1997, Richard decided to call

Nick, but even then things were not that simple. He was given Nick's number at his flat in Wigan, but there was never an answer. He tried Nick's mother's but found no joy there either. Finally, he tracked him down at a friend's.

'To ring him, I had to be humble,' Richard later recalled in *Q*. 'It wasn't a case of ringing him up and saying, "Hey man, what the fuck are you doing with your life?" I knew that he'd probably been making his own life beyond the band. So I had to approach it being humble. If he interpreted it as eating shit, that's his head. I called him because I admire him and I want him to be with us. I didn't expect him to just drop everything and do it. I thought he might say "no".' At one point in the conversation, Richard declared that if Nick did say 'no', then he would stop writing music altogether. He also said, 'The thing is, I love Nick McCabe, and I never want to be in a band if he's not playing the guitar.' Nick did not say 'no'. The Verve were back.

'To ring him, I had to be humble. It *wasn't* a case of ringing him up and saying, "Hey man, *what* the fuck are you doing *with* your life?"'

Nick later admitted that the night before Richard phoned he had enjoyed a nice dream about having his job back at the surveyor's office where he had been training before joining the band, happy in the security and routine. Now, however, he felt he had much more perspective, telling the press, 'I've just got a life outside of it, whereas I didn't before. If anything went wrong, that was my day. And now I've got a balance where the two feed off each other.'

The rumour circulated that Richard had actually decided to call Nick after his psychic adviser – apparently a member of the Spiritualist Church near his London home – told him it was time to do so. Whatever the facts, The Verve had reformed. In the immediate aftermath, both Richard and Nick seemed very happy, and open to discussing their previous difficulties. Although Richard admitted that 'things got pretty volatile, although never physically', he now felt that he and Nick were solid: 'Since then, me and Nick communicate better than we've ever done in our lives. Me and Nick are mates at the end of the day, mates that lost the plot with each other. Something was guiding us through all these bizarre places we've been in the last eighteen months.'

For Nick, the return of the band capped what had been a bizarre period of his life. At their first rehearsal with the newly reunited group he said he felt 'like a sixteen-year-old again . . . amazing. I've benefited most out of this, really, 'cos I've got a sense of whatever goes wrong doesn't really matter, 'cos I fell to the bottom and it wasn't so bad.' Their mutual respect was put on public display when Nick appeared to take all the blame for the split, saying, 'I fucked it up, really. It was me. It was me on my own. I have mental problems!' Richard would not have it, retorting in *NME* how 'he might have had problems – we all had problems. But I didn't have empathy. Didn't have life experience enough to be able to cushion and deal with it. I have now.'

When questioned why he had reformed without Nick only weeks after the split, Richard seemed to want to deny this ever really happened, and undoubtedly there was an element of the reunited friends trying to rewrite their own history. Either way, the shock of the split, and the fumblings in the aftermath, seemed to have served a purpose. 'By not being *in* a group,' Richard explained to journalist Tom Lanham, 'I've learned a lot *about* the group, the power of the group, the power of us all individually and together, and that none of us is greater than the sum total. I've learned that we ain't just this one-dimensional thing, that our brains and our psyches and our personalities are very complex things. And to me, the rest of my life, the rest of my musical career will be based on searching that part of your brain that a lot of people like to keep nice and quiet, thank you very much. Because if they tap into it, life becomes a bit rocky. I don't need no shrink. I don't need no fuckin' pills to make me .. . I'm fortunate, because I do have music.' He also said, tellingly, 'I know today that I did the right thing. We wouldn't be here now if we hadn't split.'

The reunion was announced in the music papers immediately, in a press release from a Verve spokeswoman that announced, 'The Verve never really went away. Nick left, but they didn't split up. Nick has now rejoined and the album is underway. The album sounds wonderful, it's going to be the best yet. It's phenomenal. I think this could be The Verve's year, definitely.'

The Verve minus Nick had virtually got the finished album in the bag, but with the guitarist now joining the sessions with Youth and Chris Potter, Richard insisted that completed tracks be reworked. By this stage, Chris Potter was really masterminding the sessions, with Youth taking a back seat. Immediately, the band's former chemistry returned, and Richard described the feeling as like 'slipping into a pair of old corduroys'. Jams started to feature again, squeezing in past Youth's disciplined regime, with Potter allowing them to write much more groove-orientated material in this fashion. Nick soon came up with a new track, 'Catching The Butterfly', based almost entirely around some guitar effects he was fiddling with, which was completed in a half-hour jam. In all, the newly reunited band created another six songs, after which the album was ready. With the master tapes completed, The Verve booked their first UK dates for almost two years, scheduling an opening at Sheffield Leadmill on 14 June 1997. The return single, 'Bitter Sweet Symphony' was pencilled in for release just two days later.

'I never got to the point *where* I was truly up for it, to be honest. For one I *was* in the middle of finishing the record, so you've got to look after your energy levels, and two, I was *very* ill. Everyone else apart from me *was* gagging for it . . .'

Then, with appallingly bad timing, 'The Verve voodoo', as the band call it, struck again. Richard was taken ill, and was ordered by his doctor to rest for a minimum of six weeks. The comeback tour was cancelled at the eleventh hour. Recording the new album had taken its toll on Richard, despite the more leisurely approach, and emotionally and physically he was still shattered. Apparently, the lymph glands in his neck had swollen to 'the size of footballs'. In rehearsals the mellower tunes were okay, but as soon as the more rocky numbers began, he was in excruciating pain every time he tried to sing. Realising this, and with the stakes so high on the

Opposite: The Verve triumphant. 1997 was their comeback year, with the big hits
'Bitter Sweet Symphony' and 'The Drugs Don't Work'.

return tour, he decided he could not take the risk and abandoned the dates. When the *NME* asked him about this disastrous start to The Verve's return, he said, 'I never got to the point where I was truly up for it, to be honest. For one I was in the middle of finishing the record, so you've got to look after your energy levels, and two, I was very ill. Everyone else apart from me was gagging for it . . . Whatever it takes wasn't there. And what we do is just too big to go out there at anything less than 100 per cent.' He went on, 'Mentally I've been at Def Con One for fucking two years and it takes its toll. And if you're physically not up for it as well then you've just got nothing left at all. I've said it before . . . we're on the edge in this fuckin' band. There's no point fuckin' kidding. It was always gonna be like this. A lot of other lead singers would have done that tour. They'd have shuffled the songs around and got through it, because they would have either been scared not to do it or outside pressures would have made them do it. But I think people deserve more than having me at

'Mentally I've been at Def Con One for fucking *two* years and it takes its toll. And if you're physically not up for it as *well* then you've just got nothing left at all. I've said it before . . . *we're* on the edge in this fuckin' band. There's no point fuckin' kidding.'

40 per cent. It's been too long, you know what I'm saying? Why fuck around now?'

Rumours sprang up that Richard was suffering from drug problems again, that the old trusty 'nervous exhaustion' which the industry uses to cover a multitude of sins was about to be trotted out again. In actual fact, 'a viral infection' was blamed. The Verve strenuously denied the rumours and rescheduled the dates for August. It was no more than The Verve voodoo about which they had joked about throughout their career: the cancelled Glastonbury show due to Pete breaking his foot, the amps blowing up during live transmissions, Nick snapping his finger, and now this cancelled tour. Sobbo's theory was that it was due to all the dark things they had done with drugs. No one else wished to speculate, but few would argue. And the voodoo was not finished yet . . .

*   *   *

While they had been away, Britpop had faded away, leaving in its wake the supergroup Oasis, the newly hardcore Blur, an absent Elastica, and a host of also-rans who now sounded painfully dated. The Prodigy had taken the charts by the jugular with their Number 1 singles 'Firestarter' and 'Breathe', going on to become only the seventh British band ever to chart at Number 1 in the American *Billboard* album charts with *The Fat Of The Land*. The Chemical Brothers, Underworld and other loosely similar acts had created a clumsily titled 'electronica' movement that some said was about to overthrow rock 'n' roll. Jarvis Cocker's Pulp had lost Russell Senior and struggled to retain some of the form and profile they had finally enjoyed. Even Richard's former astral rantings had been cheaply hijacked by Kula Shaker. The disappointing Seahorses, the cocky but mundane Cast, and a recycled but pretentious Paul Weller completed what was, after Britpop's momentary brilliance, a very ordinary gathering. Richard, although frustrated by his absence, saw nothing to frighten him: 'I don't think we really missed out on much being away. The last eighteen months haven't been the most colourful fucking period in English music have they?' More seriously, he instantly set The Verve's stall out, reaching for the same lofty ambitions that they had previously held, telling *NME*, 'We need to start setting new standards. Make 1997 Year Zero. People say rock 'n' roll's dead. Is it fuck! It's just that people's imaginations have died.' He went on, 'The ultimate crime is not to stimulate yourself or other people, and then you get some spotty little student singing Kinks songs on *The Chart Show*. But it only sets it up better for people who are actually doing the business. And this time they're listening.'

to the top

'*People are realising what they've been missing – a crucial English band.*'
david boyd

'*We've been listening to "Bitter Sweet Symphony" for the last six months thinking, "What are people gonna make of this tune?"*'
richard ashcroft

The first Verve single for nearly two years, 'Bitter Sweet Symphony', was a comeback of startling brilliance. From the opening, jabbing strings to the climactic finale, the song was an extraordinary, euphoric hymn to pre-millennium life. As Richard's vocals soar to new heights, the band's juddering, gyroscopic rhythm and delicate guitar work provide a truly magnificent backdrop, with the entire track soaked in fabulous string arrangements. Richard sings of being 'a million different people from one day to the next' and 'I'll take you down the only road I've ever been down', reminding us of the extreme journey the band have already made. It is an ode to the futility of existence, not entirely original, but nevertheless completely convincing. 'Bitter Sweet Symphony' sounds like the musical healing of all The Verve's past troubles in one song.

The release was all the more impressive for the glowing, beautiful ballads on the B-side, 'Lord I Guess I'll Never Know' and 'So Sister', which simply reinforced the notion that The Verve were back bigger and better than ever. From the depths of 1995 to such sheer class was a truly amazing transformation.

As if the song was not strong enough on its own, the video for 'Bitter Sweet Symphony' was a classic as well, and would go on to be nominated for, and win, scores of awards. Richard is seen walking down a street, staring straight ahead at some indeterminate point, singing the song, bumping into anyone who strays across his path, including ladies with shopping bags, cars, even old-aged pensioners and bikers. At the end of the street, he is joined by the rest of the band, who continue on their path unfettered. The sheer arrogance, the determination, the focus – it was all perfectly The Verve.

It was filmed over two days during the final sessions for the forthcoming third album, when the band were camped out at Maison Rouge Studios, behind Chelsea Football Club's Stamford Bridge home. The street Richard is seen walking down is actually Hoxton Street in east London. Directed by Walter Stern, the video was a strong complement to the tremendous comeback single. Stern's previous work had included the startling 'Firestarter' and 'Breathe' promos for the Prodigy.

Despite this, Richard and the band were always reluctant to get too involved in videos: 'I never want to get involved in that circus,' he told *Scotland On Sunday*. 'It takes away what we're really about, which is music. I think that video we did compromised that a little bit for me. I think an attitude came across, but you gotta be careful what you give to people. You can sometimes go beyond the music itself. When that happens it's a tragedy.' Few people agreed, as the video found itself on heavy rotation on MTV and aired on all major pop shows. Richard did, however, acknowledge the thought that had been put into the promo clip: 'It's my life, that's what I'm here for. I'm not talking like I'm Jesus or something, but I've been waiting to do it and I'm prepared for it. That's why the video had me walking down the road, y'know, because that's my life.'

The hype surrounding the single started weeks before the actual release. BBC Radio 1's Jo Whiley made it her Single of the Week five weeks before launch, and the next week Breakfast DJ Mark Radcliffe did the same.

NME put them on the front cover, and *Melody Maker* duly made it their Single of the Week as well, saying 'Talk about a fucking comeback.' *NME* went on to say, 'We are witnessing no mere re-formation here, but rather an authentic rock 'n' roll rebirth – "Bitter Sweet Symphony" is the most

'The *Verve*'s absence, apart from redefining the band's own sense of direction, had enshrined them in the history of rock as a great but failed group. Thus, *when* they returned it *was* an unexpected, and heartily received, second chance.'

incredible record released by a British rock band this year. At the very least.' By release date, there was a tangible feeling that something *big* was about to happen.

Suspicions were confirmed the following Sunday when The Verve crashed into the charts at Number 2, kept off the top spot only by the pseudo-cover of the Police's 'Every Breath You Take' by Puff Daddy, a tribute song he had penned for murdered rapper Notorious B.I.G, one of the year's biggest selling singles. The Verve had never competed on this level before. Alongside the chart position, there was a general feeling that this was a final, justifiable success for a band whose legend had swelled since they split up. The Verve's absence, apart from redefining the band's own sense of direction, had enshrined them in the history of rock as a great but failed group. Thus, when they returned it was an unexpected, and heartily received, second chance. In the light of Noel Gallagher's continual flattery of the band during their break from the business, by the time they re-formed it was almost as if in the interim they had been far more famous and revered than they ever had been when they were together. That the band came back at Number 2 was proof of this view, and the fifteen weeks on the chart for the single suggested it was no flash in the pan. As the summer of 1997 matured, and 'Bitter Sweet Symphony' could be heard blasting out of car radios, workplaces and shop windows all over the country, it became perhaps *the* defining single of the summer.

The response wasn't just in Britain – the single went on to reach the Top 3 in Italy, earned a gold record in Ireland, hit the Top 10 in Thailand and Turkey, and even reached Number 2 in Saudi Arabia. The band were stunned, although not unduly surprised – they knew the song was good, and were now pleased about its impact: 'It's now one of those songs that has taken on a life of its own,' Richard beamed. He was delighted that the forthcoming album would now be heard by a massive audience: 'We've taken on five times the amount of people that we had eighteen

'Basically . . . *we* took a bit of string and a bit of bongo and built . . . the . . . fucking . . . symphony . . around it. *W*ith an orchestra, *w*ith *v*arious tracks of guitars, fucking *v*ocals, feedback, bells, the lot and made this inspiring piece of music.'

months – even seven weeks – ago with one song. There's people pulling up to me in cars while I'm walking down the street going, "Oi, mate, the video's finished, y'know?!" It's mad.'

Unfortunately, things could never be that simple. As if The Verve voodoo was feeling left out, disaster struck. Four days before 'Bitter Sweet Symphony' had been released, the band's management had received a fax from the legendary and highly powerful American lawyer and one-time manager of the Rolling Stones, Allen Klein. In it, he notified The Verve that samples in the song were in breach of certain publishing rights, and therefore demanded any royalties from the single's sales. As Klein owned the back catalogue to the early Stones music, he had the legal right. The sample in question, a string and bell loop taken from an instrumental version of 'The Last Time' found on an Andrew Loog Oldham album of Stones songs, was not, as commonly perceived, the defining string section of The Verve's song, but nevertheless featured in it. Klein threatened an injunction preventing sales of the song, and pulling the single and removing it from the album was considered, but this was highly undesirable so the band had to concede. At first they thought they would lose just half of the cash, but eventually, they received not one penny. Ironically, Jagger and Richards had heard the track and were said to like it, but refused to get involved in the argument.

Richard was gutted: 'At the moment, I'm too pissed off to even fucking talk about that situation,' he frothed in *NME*. 'Basically . . . we took a bit of string and a bit of bongo and built . . . the . . . fucking . . . symphony . . . around it. With an orchestra, with various tracks of guitars, fucking vocals, feedback, bells, the lot and made this inspiring piece of music and got it fucking taken away for legal reasons.' He went on to say in the press, 'It's horrible and it's a pisser and it's a downer, but it's beautiful because the song goes, "You're a slave to the money then you die". In the end, who gives a shit? There's more to be had from this band than "Bitter Sweet Symphony". We'll make another fucking symphony.' He said the debacle had made him think twice about listening to a Rolling Stones record again, and defended his band's achievement, saying, 'I'm not bitter about it, money ain't everything, but credit is important, where it's due, and Jagger and Richards haven't written a tune as good as that for fucking twenty years . . . "Bitter Sweet Symphony" was written by The Verve, everyone who's heard it knows that, so that's it.' His last word on the entire sham was: 'As far as I'm concerned it's one of the greatest songs ever made.'

This disappointment would come back to haunt The Verve in the first few months of 1998, when Nike proposed to use 'Bitter Sweet Symphony' for an advertising campaign. The track had been chosen as *Rolling Stone* magazine's 'Single of the Year, 1997', and The Verve's management had been inundated with requests by huge firms to use it in their advertisements. With allegations about the working conditions of Nike's overseas workers, and their general corporate image, The Verve would not ordinarily have even thought twice before declining the offer. However, with Klein owning the publishing rights, they effectively had no control over the decision. This meant that Klein's publishing company, Abko, could legally re-record the music for commercial purposes and people still might think it was The Verve. The band finally agreed to allow Nike use of the track for a limited period of three months in America, in the hope that this 'would deter all other possible usage of the song', and because of Nike's 'consistent history of tasteful and creative advertising campaigns'. The band also announced that any monies that might come their way from this advert would go to the magazine to help the homeless, the *Big Issue,* The British Red Cross Landmines Appeal and Youth 2000. The Verve will always have the last laugh, as well, on this story – on the sleeve artwork for *Urban Hymns,* they placed a letter they had received from Andrew Loog Oldham, saying how much he loved the track and that 'the Stones were probably too old to remember where they nicked that particular riff from themselves'.

*   *   *

The re-forming of the band did not put an end to the rumours, which now had it that Nick had left again. A spokesman for the band laughed this off, and blamed it on 'bored people in the industry'. In reality The Verve reinforced their new solidity by playing a series of dates in the summer of 1997 that confirmed what many have described as 'the comeback of the decade'. The Reading Festival was particularly poignant, as this was the scene of the original Second Coming that never was, when the Stone Roses' pitiful performance put paid to their reputation. Whereas the critics had destroyed the Roses at a vicious press conference, The Verve got on with the business of giving inspiring live shows. Although relegated from the main stage to one of the tents to make way for Metallica and Marilyn Manson ('Imagine watching the main stage when you could be here, watching us!'), and with 'Bitter Sweet Symphony' proving to have less impact live than on record, The Verve's live show was nevertheless back at full tilt. Supported by Simon Tong's additional keyboards, the epic grandeur that The Verve had always possessed in performance (even if erratically) was in evidence more than ever. Richard, strutting around the stage with his so-called 'pimp roll', was as cocky as ever. As one reviewer at the gig said, 'They've talked a magnificent fight for years, while not quite fulfilling all the propaganda and potential. Now though, everything is right.'

If 'Bitter Sweet Symphony' had shown The Verve to be first-rank songwriters, their next single, 'The Drugs Don't Work' left the competition in its wake. It was, quite simply, one of the all-time great ballads. Coming after 'Bitter Sweet Symphony', the stakes were extremely high, but the lush follow-up single surpassed even its predecessor – Noel Gallagher's often inflated declarations were, this time at least, justified when he called the song 'mind-blowing'. With a 40-piece orchestra, gentle acoustic strumming, impassioned vocals, and heart-rending lyrics, it was a stunning piece of work. The lines 'And if you wanna show, then just let me know/And I'll sing in your ear again' were particularly beautiful, proof positive that Richard's lyrics had evolved beyond recognition since the early days of his pretentious ramblings. 'To me that tune's about total love, it says, "Love, I'm fucked up, but I'll go anywhere with you." There's lines in there that are personal to me and personal to someone close to me and I can't really go into that side of things too much.'

Anticipation over the single was immense, and a controversy with *The Chart Show* did little to temper this. The Verve, who had recently been showing a few signs of childish arrogance, informed the popular Saturday television show that the video for the new single could only be shown in its entirety, without any of the pop-up computer style menus that are a central feature of the programme. Obviously surprised by such a request, especially as no other bands, Oasis included, opposed their format, the *Chart Show* refused. The Verve admonished them in the press and the show's producers refused to budge. The puerile and rather pretentious stand by The Verve did, however, help to create even more publicity for the single. All the same, some observers wondered if the success was going to Richard's head.

This mattered little when 'The Drugs Don't Work' crashed into the charts in the first week of September at Number 1. The publicity campaign, masterminded by industry heavyweight Scott Piering, had ensured the record's success. In the week of release, the song was played 1,200 times on British radio alone. However, the glory was short-lived, as the following week the biggest-selling single of all time was released, Elton John's 'Candle In The Wind '97' his tribute to the late Princess Diana, who had died on 31 August, sending the country into a massed national mourning. This did little to dampen The Verve's spirits – when asked what it felt like to be Number 1, Richard pompously said in the *News Of The World,* 'I suppose I was thrilled, which I was, but it worried me because I never wanted to appeal to young kids. Our music isn't innocent or superficial and I don't like to think of all those kids listening to some of our darker tracks.' This patronising attitude would rear its head again later in the year, when he went even further, saying he didn't want teenagers even buying his records. This was, of course, utter conceit, and there was no sign of The Verve discouraging these sales in the record shops. It was also a shame to taint what was a beautiful piece of music with such ludicrous pronouncements.

There was some degree of debate about the song's subject-matter. On one level, it appeared to be about a seriously ill person and their loved one sitting by them, declaring their undying love. Yet Richard was also happy to focus on the narcotic interpretation of the song, which inevitably many of the papers emphasised. When *NME* asked him about this, he said, 'That song is another barrier being broken, what it's saying is that you don't have to jump up and down on *Top Of The Pops* and tell people that life is sweet . . . it's a chance to say something a bit more cutting . . . drugs are part of our culture. It's part of our vocabulary, no-one hardly even mentions the word "drugs" these days in songs.' He continued: 'I see "Drugs Don't Work" as a love song. Not about drugs not working but about being that far down and you realise that they're not getting you to where they used to. Don't get me wrong though, I'm not doing a Nancy Reagan and saying, "Don't do it." Whatever gets you through the night, that's fine by me. I'm just saying that we've been there, y'know, and I think a lot of other people in our generation have been too. It's not like some fuckin' *Grange Hill* version of life.' His final comment was '"Drugs Don't Work" is up there with some of my all-time greats . . .' He was not alone in that opinion.

The rise of The Verve to the top spot in the UK meant that Richard began to experience a few of the negative sides of fame, things that his friend Noel had by now become used to. A good example is how, shortly after they hit Number 1, the tabloids announced an 'exclusive' story of how he and Kate Radley from Spiritualized were having a 'wild affair', when they had in fact been married for two years. At the Phoenix Festival, the 'celebrity couple' even made it to the gossip columns, but Richard was far from flattered by all the attention, warning *Vox*: 'I love Kate, that's it, that's all I've got to say about it . . . If anyone tries to demean anyone in the situation, in print, they'll be getting a fucking baseball bat over the head from me, simple as that. I'm not here to be fucking . . . analysed. I shouldn't have to deal with it. That's the hardest thing to deal with in all this, without a fucking doubt.'

* * *

The week preceding the release of The Verve's third album, they played three nights supporting Oasis at the massive Earls Court in west London. With Oasis's third album, *Be Here Now*, having generally been received rather tepidly by the critics, many people felt this was The Verve's chance to snatch the Gallaghers' slipping crown. For the bands themselves, there was little such rivalry; instead they saw it as a triumph over adversity, as Richard gushed in *Vox*: 'The great thing about it is Liam and Noel, me and this lot [the band] we've all done it. Done a line, played in front of 200 people together, said we'd be the biggest bands in the world when we meant nothing and, three-and-a-half years later, go on in front of 20,000 people. Talk about a fuckin' celebration. Dream material. They've done it before, but I still think us being with them there makes it even better. And every fucker in that room's gonna know who we are as well, it's not 200 people at the front, bored. We're gonna go on to "Bitter Sweet Symphony", full orchestra, and it's gonna be . . . The Verve and Oasis.'

Unfortunately, it wasn't 200 people at the front bored, it was 20,000. The Verve were on stage at the ridiculous time of 7 p.m., while most fans were still travelling to the gig, and despite The Verve's recent chart success, the crowd was so strongly partisan towards Oasis that The Verve had to work really hard for recognition, especially for the previously un-aired tracks from *A Northern Soul*. Before the gig, Richard had declared, 'People are gonna see us for the first time and for them it's gonna be like seeing *The Godfather* or *Apocalypse Now* for the first time on a musical level, something that's gonna shake 'em.' Maybe it did not work out like that, but the fact that The Verve were there at all was a tribute to their perseverance and talent.

the best of 1997

'I was on the train the other day and these people were stood on the platform waitin' for my carriage to go past, wavin' and shoutin'. That was great. It was like, "You know who I am and you're into the records, and you're giving us a salute." And I'm goin', "Yeah!"'
richard ashcroft

'I'm mates with Terry from Brookside, is that any good? He helped me move my piano into the flat.'
richard ashcroft

On 29 September 1997, The Verve released their third, highly anticipated album, *Urban Hymns*. The depth and scope of this album easily surpassed their previous work. Claims had been made that *A Northern Soul* was a 'lost classic', but in the light of this new work, that view had to be revised. Where the second album was now clearly overambitious and pompous, *Urban Hymns* aimed high and, in the case, made it. It was a long album, at just over 70 minutes, and towards the end this dissipated the focus, with some of the band's traditional wanderings taking the shine off their feat, but certainly the first half of the album was a genuine masterpiece of emotional ferocity and delicate melody.

Encasing the record was another stylish sleeve by Brian Cannon, this time an informal shot of the band sitting in Richmond Park, actually taken when they were waiting for the photography lighting to be set up. (A Verve fan has declared on the Internet that if you analyse the skyline, Richard's hat and the trees in the picture, the word 'love' is clearly, and deliberately, visible.) This was intentionally their simplest sleeve yet, with Richard saying 'just listen to the fucking record'.

'Bitter Sweet Symphony' makes a massive opener, but in some ways it raises the stakes so high as to demand the extraordinary of the rest of the work. The bruising 'Rolling People' is a reminder that The Verve are not averse to rocking out, this track standing out all the more for being surrounded by three of the nineties' finest musical moments: 'The Drugs Don't Work' and the beautiful account of new love, 'Sonnet', as well as 'Bitter Sweet Symphony'. This neo-psychedelia was repeated by a number of occasional throwbacks to the old Verve, but they do not always work as well as the new material. An example of this is 'Catching The Butterfly', full of swirling discordant noises and shuffling beats, which struggles to throw off the musty, mystical flavour it inevitably creates, not helped in its task by repetitive and unimaginative lyrics like 'My lucid dreams/ My forgotten schemes.' This track might perhaps have been more at home on *A Storm In Heaven.*

The tempo is slowed right down with the next track, 'Neon Wilderness', which ends the excellent opening volley. In a pseudo-Jeff Buckley style, the song creeps through a maze of odd guitar warbles and repetitious rhythmic spats, hypnotising and drawing the listener in. Shame about the title. Next up is the heartbreaking 'Space And Time', one of many mentions on the album of failed love affairs. Elegant strumming, ragged electric guitar snatches, beautiful keyboards and backing vocals make this yet another emotionally lush track, although the rather clichéd chorus spoils things somewhat. Still, the sadness remains all-pervading: 'We feel numb because we don't see/That if we really cared/And we really loved/Think of all the joy we'd share.'

The melancholia continues with the rather average 'Weeping Willow', which sounds unnervingly close to Oasis, in particular 'Wonderwall' and 'Champagne Supernova'. Maybe all those hazy nights on tour with the Gallagher brothers had rubbed off on them. 'Lucky Man' revels confidently in a string-laden buoyancy, with gentle guitar riffs and acoustic backing that recapture the heights of the opening four songs – Richard seems much more at ease with himself as he sings 'I'm standing naked/Smiling, I feel no disgrace/With who I am.' The eternal love expressed on 'One Time' is emotionally appealing also, but the track sounds too derivative and competes with its immediate predecessor. 'This Time' is an odd, almost misplaced throwback to 1989, all shuffling drums, spoken vocals, attitude and Squire-ish guitars.

'You've got to open up yourself and that's *why* lyrically, after five years, I've opened up on this *new* album. I've learned to take *away* the bullshit, get rid of the excess imagery.'

The album's momentum is falling by now, and 'Velvet Morning' does little to reset the balance, with its Echo And The Bunnymen guitars and stuttered beats failing to excite, resembling a weak Neil Young more than The Verve firing on all cylinders (although it does contain the excellent line 'I was born a little damaged man'). Then the crassly titled 'Come On!', a primitive tribute to Richard's habit of continually shouting this phrase off mike on stage, closes the album in an improvised, apocalyptic gesture of defiance. As Richard put it: 'The album ends very deliberately on a positive, assured . . . ahem, "Fuck You." That is the "fuck you" of a man who's on top of it, who's buzzing, who's got those guitars raging underneath him. It's a "fuck you" of total joy.' It is a return to form, with searing guitars, dance rhythms and compelling screamed vocals. Then a closing, hidden and unnamed track mixes soft guitar jangles with an infant's squeals, in an odd conclusion to the album.

Vocally, this was undoubtedly Richard Ashcroft's finest work to date. On the calmer acoustic numbers, his voice is drenched with emotion; on the rockier songs, his ability to thrash around and scream rock 'n' roll has few equals. Thematically, the self-analytical lyrics were venturing into new territory for him: 'You've got to open up yourself,' he revealed to *Melody Maker*, 'and that's why lyrically, after five years, I've opened up on this new album. I've learned to take away the bullshit, get rid of the excess imagery. Sometimes you can hide behind words and I think I've got to go through a process of getting to the point where I don't need to hide any more. Why hide? A lot of us are going through similar emotions at the same time, it's just that we all have different ways of dealing with them. If you go to work you switch them off for nine, ten hours of the day, but when you get home at 11 o'clock it all gets on top of you because you have to put a block on it. With music I'm allowed . . . it's one of the few things in life that you can actually fuck all that bullshit.'

'*Why* hide? A lot of us are going through similar emotions at the same time, it's just that *we* all have different *ways* of dealing *with* them.'

With the focus on love across much of the album, it is also clear that he was very happy in his marriage to Kate Radley, implying that he had found that special relationship: 'It's something we're all searching for and you can definitely find it one-on-one with someone. There are moments and times together when you can really elevate yourself beyond thinking about death or how shite the world is.'

When asked to sum up the album's lyrical core, Richard explained it thus: 'This record is about recognising in myself that I am not this one-dimensional character. Sometimes musicians artists and writers try to paint themselves as this one "self" and I think I'm a very fragmented, mixed up . . . like we all are. It's about admitting it, I'm not perfect, in some instances in my life I can be a complete shit. It's not something I'm proud of, it's something you've got to face at some point and say, "Right, how do I make it better, how do I move on?"'

One element of *Urban Hymns* that in many ways stands in direct opposition to Richard's declarations that he could not function musically without Nick is the fact that the record's strongest moments are all tracks that he wrote alone during the hiatus before the band re-formed. The classic anthems, namely 'Bitter Sweet Symphony' and 'The Drugs Don't Work', were entirely his own work. In addition, 'Sonnet' and 'Lucky

Man', the other clear winners were, also largely drawn from his solitude. When Nick returned, the songs took on a more old-style Verve form, more improvised in feel, if not in fact. To put it bluntly, The Verve's balladry is currently unparalleled, but their rockier songs are more ordinary. This may be unduly harsh on Nick, but there is a clear dividing line between the quality of the tracks on the album, and the central factor in that is Richard Ashcroft.

At the time of the album's impending release the band found it hard to contain their excitement and confidence. Just before launch day, Richard said, 'The Verve have always been one of the heaviest bands around, but there's some beautiful songs on here too. We can't wait for people to hear it. We're always going to be pushing it – that's what we're about. These songs have come together over a two-year period and when you get five people locking in like we do, the music becomes greater than the individual.'

The media's response to the album was unreserved acclaim. *Mojo* said, 'Its greatness is in its humanity and in the sense that, from fear, failure and insecurity, it's possible to scale heights in a way which not only sets the standard for the rest of the year, but the decade too.' *NME* chipped in with: 'This is the musical signature of the year for anyone not so out of love with music that they're satisfied with Elton John's bleeding heart. But *Urban Hymns* is a big, big record.' In the US, the press acclaim was similarly warm: *Alternative Press* said the album was 'simply awesome', whilst the *Carillon*'s Tricia Kuss said the 'empowering lyrics and terrific arrangements [produce] a terrific gem from the first to the last track proving that you can achieve machine gun rhythms while still having a positive outlook'. *Rolling Stone*'s John Wiederhorn concluded his review: '*Urban Hymns* is a breathtaking venture, an ambitious balance of stargazing and worldy pathos.' MTV weighed in with their hefty opinion, with Mitch Myers saying, 'This [is a] blissful reunion, a heady combination of Richard Ashcroft's evocative vocals and guitarist Nick McCabe's soulsonic reverberations which have always been at the centre of The Verve's music, and this grand tradition continues mightily on *Urban Hymns*. From the opening strains of "Bitter Sweet Symphony" to the final, crashing chords of "Come On", Ashcroft and McCabe devise a lush web of symphonic rock postures. It's nice to have The Verve back. They know how to fill a romantic void that you probably didn't even know that you had.'

The public agreed, buying the album in such quantities that it stormed into the charts at Number 1, in the process becoming the fifth fastest-selling album in the UK ever. It passed the platinum mark of 300,000 in less than two weeks and stayed at the top for many more weeks, taking up residence in the Top Five for months. Its success was all the more impressive in view of the acts that also had albums out at the same time, including a newly revitalised Elton John, the Rolling Stones, Portishead, and the Spice Girls. Even their close friends Oasis could not begin to compete with the longevity that this album enjoyed.

The album topped many magazines' end of year 'Best Of . . .' lists and

'The whole scene, all the bullshit. Having a cynical, sardonic attitude about stuff like that is difficult, 'cos you come across as an arrogant c . . t, but I'm not interested in all that. Awards and all that – who cares?'

returned to the Number 1 spot over the Yuletide period, shifting 145,000 copies in those hectic six pre-Christmas days alone. Eventually, in February 1998, *Urban Hymns* went on to sweep the Brit Awards. Although faced with extremely stiff competition from the year's other quality albums, including the epochal *OK Computer* by Radiohead and the storming monster success of the Prodigy's *The Fat Of The Land*, *Urban Hymns* swept all before it. By the end of the night, The Verve, nominated for five awards, had won Best Group, Best Album and Best Producer (along with collaborators Youth and Chris Potter). Shame they weren't there to receive the award in person (as many stars were not) – they were playing a rescheduled gig at Brixton Academy in aid of a the National Children's Homes, Action for Children, and the House Our Youth 2000 campaign. To save face for the organisers of the Brits, part of their gig was beamed via satellite into the award ceremony hall. In the light of this incredible achievement, album sales rocketed the record back to the top spot yet again. They also swept the *NME*'s Brat Awards, where Richard refused to get up on stage to receive the trophies.

The massive success of the album was reinforced in late November with the release of 'Lucky Man', the third single to be taken from *Urban Hymns*. The track hit the Number 7 spot, again with almost universal radio play, and this confirmed (ironically for a band who had previously put out ten-minute records) that The Verve had been *the* singles band of 1997.

Towards the end of the year, Richard informed the media that he would no longer be readily available for interviews. He was tired of the media circus, and fed up with having to explain, defend and justify himself. (Radiohead's Thom Yorke did the same at this time also.) This, his attitude towards teenagers buying his records, and his refusal to attend glitzy award ceremonies led to many people denouncing him as arrogant, but this was an accusation he was used to: 'The whole scene, all the bullshit. Having a cynical, sardonic attitude about stuff like that is difficult, 'cos you come across as an arrogant cunt, but I'm not interested in all that. Awards and all that – who cares?'

After the Brat Awards, which were only voted for by the public, Richard expressed more of his concerns about these industry ceremonies: 'The reason I'm here tonight is because people have voted, it's not voted by an industry, it's not voted by anyone who wants the album to sell a bit more for their own purposes. I think any other award system is an absolute farce, but I'm happy to be here because I know there's people out there that have put a cross on a piece of paper and I'm here to say, "Thanks a lot. Nice one. Thanks to everyone who voted for us."' Interestingly, no-one called him Mad Richard that night.

tomorrow the *world*

'I was talking to someone who saw Led Zeppelin play here in the early seventies who said it was fucking amazing, but it'll be the same tonight. We'll take the fucking roof off this place.'
richard ashcroft

The world tour for *Urban Hymns* compounded the success of the album in the UK. In Europe, their early 1998 tour sold out in a less than two hours, and album sales across the continent were tremendous, pushing *Urban Hymns* past the 2.5 million mark by mid-January (worldwide the figures passed the four million mark in April 1998).

Life on the road for The Verve this time was far more civilised. Although no-one claimed to be exactly puritanically clean, there was none of the band-threatening excess of previous years. Richard first went on a two-week holiday in Majorca, where he ate a strict 'no toxins' diet and slept for long hours, in order to best prepare him physically for the forthcoming tour. In addition, the management had scheduled the dates realistically, so that the band had a reasonable chance of staying on top of things. Behind the band each night, as if to remind them to stay calm, was a series of platitudes beamed in bright lights up against the backdrop, with slogans such as 'Think that you are somebody and you'll be somebody', 'A psychotic is just a guy who's found out what's going on', and 'Virtue is not photogenic'.

Although 1997 had been a triumphant year for the band, it was a strangely muted time for their live shows. Many of their gigs in that twelve-month spell were very average – the tour cancellation was obviously not an ideal start. Glastonbury was very warmly received: *Melody Maker* (now back firmly behind the band) said it gave us 'unique glimpses into another world' (and at least Nick's amp did not blow up), but the Earls Court dates, partly due to the unreasonably early start, were not exactly earth-shattering shows either. Perhaps their preparation – they did not rehearse in the traditional sense, but played all-night jams – had let the Verve down.

The musical division that rent the album between classic and average could also be seen on the live dates. The *Observer*'s Barbara Ellen picked up on this when she reviewed the band's Hammersmith Palais gig in the late summer: 'Brilliant, unnerving, inspired and ridiculous . . . while the rest of The Verve seem determined to resurrect the bad old days of shoe-gazing, Ashcroft bounds across the stage like a self-igniting firework.' While Richard prowled the stage barefoot on his Persian rug (now embossed with The Verve's logo – he slipped his shoes off even for the soundcheck), Nick fiddled with his effects rack and guitar, often lost in the mix, motionless at the side of his hyperactive colleague. Some observers said the two never looked at each other, there were rumours that their relationship was merely civil, and a few people tried to whip up a 'Verve to split' controversy, especially in the US. One kid was heard outside a New England gig excitedly telling his friends, 'I hear they're on different tour buses already. That's because Richard doesn't need to travel with the band. He flew into Boston all by himself . . . he's super rich!' The band, however, had heard these kinds of rumours before, and they knew this would always happen. Their main concern, or Richard's at least, was the profile they were now attracting, and he once again raised this rather silly point that 'you can't ban thirteen-year-olds from your gigs, but really I don't want to play these songs to people who aren't old enough to know what they are about. And I don't know that I'm ready to be a sex symbol.' On the same subject, he said elsewhere in the press: 'I have got conflict in my mind, though . . . I wanna write these songs. I wanna get people to listen to them. Then I'm thinking, "Do they really understand them? Do they really get into them? What level are they taking them on?" 'Cos I remember sittin' in the Viper Room a few weeks ago and there was a tape on. And I was thinkin', "I don't want my music played in this club.

Richard Ashcroft gives Rome a blast of his customary enthusiasm and self-regard during the 1998 European tour.

I don't want people with silicon tits and silicon ears listening to us.'" Still, the fans did not seem to care – on the Glasgow Barrowlands date before the album's release, 900 ticketless kids tried to storm the venue, and on London dates, touts were regularly pricing single tickets at upwards of £100 each.

Although The Verve's US success paled in comparison to that of other high-profile British acts such as Oasis, Spice Girls and the Prodigy, charting at only Number 63 in the *Billboard* listings, the album's constant presence in the Top 75, complemented by several jaunts across the States, provided a healthy platform for The Verve to progress from. Their November 1997 dates were rapturously received by many a baseball-cap-wearing crowd. Take this extract from *Rolling Stone*: 'Lead guitarist Nick McCabe played most of the show with chin on chest or back to the audience, crafting great, breathing walls of sound. Amid all the noise, though, the band still found a way to display more personality than ever before. As "Come On" faded, Ashcroft gave a thumbs-up to the crowd and McCabe, dropping his still-buzzing guitar into the hands of a roadie, lifted chin from chest and – lo and behold – smiled.'

However, the band did not help themselves by arrogantly announcing that they would be giving no press interviews in America unless it was for a cover feature. With their profile as it stood, this simply meant that instead of being strong-armed into lead interviews, the mocking magazine editors just featured someone else. For example, a prestigious feature for *Spin* magazine was turned down, and this simply went to Travis instead, with The Verve getting no coverage at all.

In addition, journalists were only allowed to talk to them about the live shows, and the band refused interviews on any other topics. All this over-inflated strategy served to do was to alienate large parts of the US media. Even the sixth-form 'anarchist' popsters Chumbawamba, who were enjoying an Indian summer to their lengthy career with their global smash 'Tubthumping', were comfortable playing more of the corporate game than this. Moreover, American audiences still called the singer Mad Richard and Captain Rock, a sign that their profile remained stuck in 1993. Nevertheless, the supportive *Rolling Stone* followed up their enthusiastic November 1997 piece with a full-length profile of the band on 16 April 1998, calling them the 'Number One rock band in England', and saying of Richard that even without his musical success 'he would still be the kind of guy who could turn heads, melt hearts, freeze rush-hour traffic and stop conversation in a vacuum-packed pub without lifting an eyebrow'.

The Verve voodoo struck again around New Year, when the band cancelled some US gigs, allegedly due to 'family bereavement' for Richard, but the exact cause was unclear. The much-anticipated spring US dates were then postponed, with a band spokesman saying it was because 'Richard wanted to get some new music out of him, some recording and some rest'. The tour was immediately rescheduled for July and August, with venues expanded from the cancelled 3,000-seaters to around 10,000 capacity halls. The eleven dates included New York's Madison Square Garden and the Bill Graham Civic Auditorium in San Francisco, as well as halls in Montreal, Houston and Seattle. Despite the initial disappointment of the winter cancelation, The Verve donated $10,000 to various charities supported by Los Angeles-based radio station KROQ. The Verve work in mysterious ways.

*   *   *

One fact that The Verve have always been keen to state in the press is the superb relationship which they have had with Hut Records. They believe that the label's willingness to let them release ten-minute singles, at the time effectively commercial suicide, was exceptionally perceptive in an industry built around the quick buck. They often berated record companies who rushed bands through their first two albums, and then slapped them on the soul-destroying and musically sterilising album-tour-album-tour treadmill. Hut had never adopted this approach and throughout the enormous success of *Urban Hymns*, it seemed that their admirable foresight was finally paying off.

However, at the start of 1998, Hut asked The Verve to put out another single from the album, an idea which the band disagreed with. Unusually, Hut pressed them on this matter, and so the band finally agreed to release 'Sonnet', but only in a format that would make it ineligible for chart recognition. Consequently, 'Sonnet' was released as part of a set of four 12-inch records on 12 March (backed by 'Stamped', 'So Sister' and 'Echo Bass'). The release was limited to just 5,000 copies, despite the huge radio coverage it received, and the official Top 40 charts refused to recognise it as a single because of the extra content, as planned. The pack was released in a cardboard mailer, and the preceding three singles from the album, all re-released on the same day, fitted into the mailer. A victory for The Verve. Apparently.

looking upwards

'We'll probably be back in the studio next year. Album out early summer. Hopefully! That's the plan. Just to keep it rolling. Because there's so many songs and ideas it would be a tragedy not to, after missing two years.'
richard ashcroft

'We've got another ten years only, probably. Once a song hasn't gone a bit further than the last, once we've hit a plateau and can't go any further up the mountain . . . that's when we'll sledge back down into obscurity.'
richard ashcroft

While *Urban Hymns* remained in the UK Top 5 and still featured strongly in album charts across the world six months after its release, The Verve set about becoming, in Richard's words, 'the new Led Zeppelin'. In this vein, they were looking to organise various huge-scale shows. They approached the Ministry of Defence with regard to playing some abandoned airfields and docks. The initial reply was that the Ministry would consider their idea and that, while George Robertson, the Defence Secretary, was himself 'not too familiar with their music,' his special adviser, Alasdair McGowan, apparently was.

the verve

One element of this new phase for The Verve was Richard's work on Mo Wax Records honcho James Lavelle's UNKLE project. This was a highly secretive and extremely credible project that was two years in the making. It was built around the legendary talent of one of the dance world's most creative forces, DJ Shadow, whose mini-album *Camel Bobsled Race* and debut long player *Endtroducing* saw him hailed as 'an experimental genius'. Also on the album were DJ Shadow with Radiohead, the Dust Brothers, the Automator, and Money Mark of Beastie Boys fame. Elsewhere, a dance track containing segments of 'Bitter Sweet Symphony', by a band called Rest Assured (the song was called 'Treat Infamy'), charted highly in the New Year, fuelling sales of *Urban Hymns* still more. The Verve even saw their success filtering through into the motor industry, when Peugeot announced a special edition of their 306 model called 'The Verve', and plastered posters for the vehicle in a somewhat similar style to the artwork for the band's 1994 compilation album *No Come Down*. The Verve understandably did not take too kindly to this and legal eagles were put in action. A spokesman for Peugeot maintained that any resemblance to the Verve's artwork was 'a happy coincidence'. Later, a reworking of 'Bitter Sweet Symphony' was used on a television advertising campaign for the new Vauxhall Astra.

Following in the footsteps of several high-profile British acts, such as Black Grape and Radiohead, who had recently released documentary-style long-format videos, The Verve announced that they too were putting out a package, provisionally entitled *This Is The Verve: Do Not Panic*. The video was shot on the band's US and UK tours in 1997, and contained live footage, interviews and backstage clips. It was filmed by George Hanson and Andy Baybutt, who had also filmed the video for 'The Drugs Don't Work', assisted by Wayne Griggs, the band's long-time friend, soundman and DJ. The band planned to release the video to the cinemas before general retail.

Musically, Richard announced that 'We're gonna do three albums in quick succession. We're on fire', a policy which was at the root of the cancelled US dates. As for any future band splits, he was confident these could be avoided: 'The thing is, all those old pressures were made by us 'cause we had our problems. They were our pressures, not the outside machine, the world. It was between us and I don't worry about it now 'cause I just know we're taking each day as it comes and having it.

Nick McCabe's delicate nervous state once more got the better of him during the 1998 tour, leading to the most recent split in the band.

We're never gonna say we're gonna be around for *x* amount of time or whatever, we're just gonna continue to do it and just get to know each other better and better and get stronger and stronger, which'll make the tunes stronger.'

The Verve were also scheduled to headline the V98 Festival on 22 and 23 August 1998, above acts that included the Seahorses, the Charlatans, Robbie Williams and Green Day. This was preceded by another massive gig on 24 May, when they played a triumphant homecoming show at Wigan's Haigh Hall, in front of an expected crowd of 33,000 people. The hall is an eighteenth-century stately home two miles outside of Wigan, and the stage was built on part of the estate's golf course – this was Wigan's first ever outdoor musical festival, and its largest ever outdoor event of any kind. In the press release for the announcement, a Verve spokesman said, 'The band have been looking for a site for a summer gig for quite a while, but as with everything they do, it had to be right and it had to be special. The site they've chosen is wonderful. The backdrop as you look beyond the stage is a quite dramatic view of Wigan. This gig is going to go down in history.' Richard also said in anticipation, 'I think that we've got that power in our sound to fill a huge space, and to still connect with people . . . we'll be able to start taking this group into its next phase.' It was pleasing to see the local authorities back the idea, especially in view of all the difficulties that Oasis had endured for their Loch Lomond and Knebworth shows. A local council spokesman, when asked about the gig, said, 'We've had a couple of letters from people living nearby who think it's a dreadful idea, but the majority think it's absolutely marvellous, especially as they're a Wigan group who are rising to the top, past the likes of Oasis and the Spice Girls.' The tickets for the gig sold out in less than 50 minutes.

The fans were not disappointed. A festival atmosphere prevailed when The Verve took to the stage at nine in the evening. Writing in the *Observer*, William Leith commented on the remarkable empathy between the band, especially Richard, and the audience: 'As Ashcroft moans and spills out his pain, the crowd watch and sway, awestruck. It's clear that they love him.' When they moved into 'The Drugs Don't Work' most of the audience sang along, not letting the song's poignant lyrics prevent them passing around their joints. The *NME*'s Victoria Segal was equally struck by how effectively the band achieved Richard's promise that they would 'connect with people'. With The Verve at their brilliant live best, this communication gave the songs a new quality, renewing them and deepening their meaning: 'for the all the undeniable anthems – the translucent purity of "The Drugs Don't Work", the incipient hysteria of "History" – the songs also take a step beyond. It's unsurprising that tonight focuses on *Urban Hymns* – not only because of the Manics-like old fans–new fans divide, but because those songs need more space to unfold. Less specifically personal, they fit a vast audience – the oilslick surge of "Catching The Butterfly", the small epiphanies of "Velvet Morning", the venomous tang of "The Rolling People". By now "Bitter Sweet Symphony" should be as pallidly commonplace as an Athena postcard, chewed up by the world of radio and advertising, yet the moment those iconic strings pitch in, it's given a whole new charge.' *Melody Maker*'s Dave Simpson concluded '"The Drugs Don't Work" confirms its status as a modern-day standard, something that will defy the ravages of time as much anything by Elvis or Bartók.'

In recognition of The Verve's new status as kings of British rock, the BBC relayed the whole set live on Radio One, and also broadcast highlights on television later that same evening, as if it were some major national sporting event.

A funny but, for Richard at least, rather disturbing event had happened two months before in March 1998, when he visited the Vatican with Kate Radley for a holiday. As he walked around the holy city, a large crowd of youngsters recognised him, and began following him 'like the Pied Piper' in and out of shops. Frustrated by the attention, he even jumped into a taxi at one stage, only to find himself being chased by two girls on a scooter. Life was clearly never going to be the same again. One final mark of The Verve's remarkable success came shortly after this experience, when the headmaster of Winstanley College announced that lunchtime gigs, which The Verve had started and had since been banned, were to be reinstated. The power of rock 'n' roll . . .

And then suddenly, almost as quickly as it had come good again, it had all gone wrong. The homecoming show at Haigh Hall was met with a warm, rather than ecstatic response. Simon Jones went missing in action first, suffering from a 'viral infection'. Rumours started to circulate that the band were arguing again, that Ashcroft was becoming a prima donna, that he was getting treated preferentially to the rest of the group. Tabloid intrusion on his married life and the articulate but outspoken interviews he was wont to give only increased the sense that the Verve *were* Richard Ashcroft. Maybe, some said, he was starting to believe this himself . . .

But the Verve have never been just one man. Ashcroft himself had, after all, famously said that without Nick McCabe the band were nothing. This was why when they originally split in 1995 the remaining members could produce nothing of worth. So it was with a odd mix of inevitability and disappointment that the news filtered through in the middle of July 1998 that McCabe had left again. Or to put it as the official statement said, he had temporarily decided not to tour for the foreseeable future, due to 'the increasing stress of touring'. The old rock 'n' roll staple of 'nervous exhaustion' was cited again, and certainly, with his difficult past, there were genuine concerns for his welfare.

Behind this, however, the rumours flew. Unsubstantiated allegations (all of them strenuously denied) circulated of a fist fight between the guitarist and the lead singer – allegedly an explosion of resentment and angst going back to 1995 when Ashcroft split the band up then effectively re-formed it without McCabe. Gossip flew around and all manner of stories existed.

In essence though, none of these theories mattered. McCabe was gone again. How would the Verve sound, or indeed survive, without him? Bravely choosing to fulfil their forthcoming touring commitments, which included fifteen dates across America, Spain and the UK, The Verve recruited the highly sought-after 60-year-old session player B. J. Cole (a steel guitarist) and headed across the Atlantic.

There was little to bolster their shattered confidence when they arrived. The 17,000-seat venue for the first date in Chicago had been downgraded to just 4,000, and that didn't sell out for a long time. Furthermore,

epilogue

the American public seemed to care little about McCabe's absence, a blessing, perhaps, but not when recognised as a symptom of their relative ignorance of the band's history. Most frustrating was the fact that the majority had come to see the band who played 'that Nike song'.

On these American dates and in front of a scowling UK crowd at V98 in Chelmsford and Leeds, The Verve, by their own lofty standards, were decidedly average. *NME*'s James Oldham said that 'you're left hoping this isn't the last time you'll see them play live. Because this was certainly no way to say goodbye.' To be fair, little else could have been expected. Hardcore Verve fans mumbled about the pointlessness of carrying on. Critics revelled in the opportunity to lampoon the stricken beast. Indeed, the music sounded mundane and the future looked very bleak.

However, The Verve are survivors. Maybe McCabe will rejoin, maybe he won't. Maybe they will split up terminally. Who can know. Indeed, even Ashcroft himself seemed unaware of McCabe's crisis, giving upbeat interviews in America whilst his own guitarist and right-hand man was packing his bags. The Verve have never been about certainties. If they do crumble, in their wake they will leave one of the great albums of recent times, plus a back catalogue of deep, dark and at times utterly inspiring music. It is a tall order for them to continue and live up to their own brilliance. Maybe they'll do it, maybe they won't. Only one thing is certain – it will be one hell of a ride finding out.

The Verve predicted they would play Madison Square Gardens (Richard did), that after three albums they would triumph (they did), and that they would earn their place in music history (they already have). What they could never have foreseen was the traumatic, disturbing, injurious and emotionally distressing path which they took to get there: the drugs, the drink, the arguments, the reconciliations, the cancellations, the near-fatal collapses and near-terminal splits. The Verve voodoo has been busy, yet somehow they have emerged stronger and more creatively brilliant for all their experiences. Perhaps they would have preferred more crazed highs than horrible lows, but maybe without them they would not have been The Verve.

discography

singles

All In The Mind/One Way To Go, 7"
4/92   Hut HUT 12

**All In The Mind/Man Called Sun/
One Way To Go, 12"**
4/92   Hut HUTT 12

**All In The Mind/One Way To Go/
Man Called Sun, CD**
4/92   Hut HUTCD 12

She's A Superstar (Edit)/Feel, 7"
6/92   Hut HUT 16

She's A Superstar/Feel, 12"
6/92   Hut HUTT 16

She's A Superstar/Feel, CD
6/92   Hut HUTCD 16

**Gravity Grave, EP (Gravity Grave[Edit]/
Endless Life/She's A Superstar
[Live at Clapham Grand 17/7/92]), 10"**
10/92   Hut HUTEN 21

**Gravity Grave, EP (Gravity Grave
[Extended Version]/Endless Life/A Man
Called Sun [Live at Clapham Grand
17/7/92]), 12"**
10/92   Hut HUTT 21

**Gravity Grave, EP (Gravity Grave
[Extended Version]/Endless Life/A Man
Called Sun [Live at Clapham Grand
17/7/92]/Gravity Grave [Encore
[Live at Clapham Grand 17/7/921], CD**
10/92   Hut HUTCD 21

**THE VERVE EP (Gravity Grave [Edit]/
A Man Called Sun/She's A Superstar
[Edit]/Endless Life/Feel), CD**
1/93   Hut HUTUS 1/YARDCD 1

**Blue/Twilight/Where The Geese Go/
No Come Down, 10"**
5/93   Hut HUTEN 29

Blue/Twilight/Where The Geese Go, 12"
5/93   Hut HUTT 29

**Blue/Twilight/Where The Geese Go/
No Come Down, CD**
5/93   Hut HUTCD 29

Slide Away/6 O'Clock, 7", pink vinyl
9/93   Hut HUT 35

**Slide Away/Make It 'Til Monday
(Acoustic)/Virtual World (Acoustic), 12"**
9/93   Hut HUTT 35

**Slide Away/Make It 'Til Monday
(Acoustic Version)/Virtual World
(Acoustic Version), CD**
9/93   Hut HUTCD 35

**This Is Music/Let The Damage Begin, 7",
burgundy vinyl**
5/95   Hut HUT 54

**This Is Music/Let The Damage Begin/
You And Me, 12"**
5/95   Hut HUTT 54

**This Is Music/Let The Damage Begin/
You And Me, CD**
5/95   Hut HUTCD 54

**On Your Own/I See The Door,
7", green vinyl**
6/95   Hut HUT 55

**On Your Own/I See The Door/
Little Gem/Dance On Your Bones, CD**
6/95   Hut HUTCD 55

On Your Own/I See The Door, cassette
6/95   Hut HUTC 55

**History (Radio Edit)/Back On My
Feet Again/On Your Own (Acoustic)/
Monkey Magic (Bralastorm Mix), CD**
9/95   Hut HUTCD 59

discography

**History (Full Version)/Grey Skies/
Life Is Not A Rehearsal, CD**
9/95ı   Hut HUTDX 59

**History (Radio Edit)/Back On My
Feet Again, cassette**
9/95   Hut HUTC 59

**Bitter Sweet Symphony (Original)/
Lord I Guess I'll Never Know/
Country Song/Bitter Sweet Symphony
(Radio Edit), CD, stickered digipak**
6/97   Hut HUTDG 82

**Bitter Sweet Symphony
(Extended Version)/ So Sister/
Echo Bass, CD digipak**
6/97   Hut HUTDX 82

**Bitter Sweet Symphony (Original)/
Lord I Guess I'll Never Know/
Country Song/Bitter Sweet Symphony
(Radio Edit), cassette**
6/97   Hut HUTC 82

**The Drugs Don't Work (Radio Edit)/
Three Steps/The Drugs Don't Work
(Demo), CD, digipak**
9/97   Hut HUTDG 88

**The Drugs Don't Work (Full Length)/
Bitter Sweet Symphony (James Lavelle
Remix)/The Crab/Stamped,
CD, digipak**
9/97   Hut HUTDX 88

**The Drugs Don't Work (Radio Edit)/
Three Steps/The Drugs Don't Work
(Demo), cassette**
9/97   Hut HUTC 88

Lucky Man/?
0/00,   Hut HUTC 00

Sonnet/?
0/00,   Hut HUTC 00

albums

A Storm In Heaven, LP gatefold sleeve
6/93   Hut HUTLP 10

A Storm In Heaven, CD
6/93   Hut CD HUT 10

Track Listing: Star Sail/Slide Away/Already There/
Beautiful Mind/The Sun, The Sea/Virtual World/
Make It 'Til Monday/Blue/Butterfly/
See You In The Next One (Have A Good Time)

NO COME DOWN export CD for U.S.A.
5/94   Hut CDHUT 18

Track Listing: No Come Down/Blue (USA Mix)/
Make It 'Til Monday (Acoustic)/
Butterfly (Acoustic)/Where The Geese Go/
Six O'Clock/One Way To Go/Gravity Grave
(Live Glastonbury '93)/Twilight

A Northern Soul, 2-LP, with inner sleeves
7/95   Hut HUTLP 27

**A Northern Soul, CD, foldout digipak
with postcard**
7/95   Hut DGHUT 27

A Northern Soul, CD
7/95   Hut CDHUT 27

Track Listing: A New Decade/This Is Music/
On Your Own/So It Goes/A Northern Soul/
Brainstorm Interlude/Drive You Home/History/
No Knock On My Door/Life's An Ocean/
Stormy Clouds/(Reprise)

**Urban Hymns, 2-LP, with inner sleeves,
outer printed mailer, 5,000 only**
9/97   Hut HUTLPX 45

Urban Hymns, CD
9/97   Hut CDHUT 45

Urban Hymns, 2-LP, with inner sleeves
10/97   Hut HUTLP 45

Track Listing: Bitter Sweet Symphony/Sonnet/
The Rolling People/The Drugs Don't Work/
Catching The Butterfly/Neon Wilderness/
Space And Time/Weeping Willow/Lucky Man/
One Day/This Time/Velvet Morning/Come On

uk promos

History, 1-track CD
8/95   Hut HUTCDP 59

**Bitter Sweet Symphony (James Lavelle
Remix)/(James Lavelle Instrumental
Remix), 12", plain white die-cut sleeve
with sticker**
6/97   Hut HUTTR 82

**Bitter Sweet Symphony (Extended
Version)/(M.S.G. Mix) (Instrumental),
12", plain white die-cut sleeve with olive
label**
6/97   Hut HUTTP 82

Bitter Sweet Symphony, 1-track CD
6/97   Hut HUTCDP 82

**The Drugs Don't Work (Radio Edit),
1-track CD, shortened title, card sleeve**
8/97   Hut HUTCDP 88

**Urban Hymns, promo CD, in gatefold
black cover with book tie**
9/97   Hut CDPHUT 45